The Revolutionary War

VOLUME 10

The Revolutionary War

VOLUME 10

An Independent Nation

James R. Arnold & Roberta Wiener

GROLIER

An imprint of

SCHOLASTIC

Scholastic Library Publishing

www.scholastic.com/librarypublishing

First published 2001 by Grolier
An imprint of Scholastic Library Publishing
Old Sherman Turnpike
Danbury, Connecticut 06816

For information address the publisher:
Scholastic Library Publishing, Old Sherman Turnpike,
Danbury, Connecticut 06816

Reprinted in 2006

Library of Congress Cataloging-in-Publication Data

The Revolutionary War.
      p. cm.
   Contents: v. 1. The road to rebellion—v. 2. The shot heard around
the world—v. 3. Taking up arms—v. 4. The spirit of 1776—v. 5.
1777: A year of decision—v. 6. The road to Valley Forge—v. 7. War of
attrition—v. 8. The American cause in peril—v. 9. The turn of the tide
—v. 10. An independent nation.
   Includes bibliographical references and indexes.
      ISBN 0-7172-5553-0 (set)—ISBN 0-7172-5554-9 (v. 1)—
ISBN 0-7172-5555-7 (v. 2)—ISBN 0-7172-5556-5 (v. 3)—
ISBN 0-7172-5557-3 (v. 4)—ISBN 0-7172-5558-1 (v. 5)—
ISBN 0-7172-5559-X (v. 6)—ISBN 0-7172-5560-3 (v. 7)—
ISBN 0-7172-5561-1 (v. 8)—ISBN 0-7172-5562-X (v. 9)—
ISBN 0-7172-5563-8 (v. 10)
      1. United States—History—Revolution, 1775–1783—Juvenile
literature. [1. united States—History—Revolution. 1775–1783.]
I. Grolier Incorporated.

E208 .R.47 2002
973.3—dc21   8947   2001018998

Printed and bound in Singapore

CONTENTS

CHAPTER ONE

DREAMING OF INDEPENDENCE 6

CHAPTER TWO

THE BRITISH IN VIRGINIA 11

CHAPTER THREE

THE NEW NATION 36

EPILOG

WHAT HAPPENED TO THEM? 60

ARMY AND NAVY RANKS
IN THE AMERICAN REVOLUTION 68

CHRONOLOGY 69

GLOSSARY 70

FURTHER RESOURCES 71

SET INDEX 72

ACKNOWLEDGMENTS 80

CHAPTER ONE

"Dreaming of Independence"

In 1780 the British had tried to win the war by invading the southern states. While the campaign in the south was taking place, the British army commander in America, General Henry Clinton, always kept a powerful force in New York City. George Washington and his army had to prevent Clinton from marching out of New York and doing harm to the rebel cause.

Washington's job was becoming harder and harder. His army had barely survived the winter of 1779-80. It had often been without food, shelter, and money. Some Connecticut regiments had even refused to obey their officers. In military language such illegal behavior was called a mutiny. During the spring and summer of 1780 the army had not accomplished anything important against the main British army in New York.

Washington explained his problems in a private letter to his brother:

"We are, during the winter, dreaming of Independence and Peace. . . . In the Spring, when our Recruits should be with the Army and in training, we have just discovered the necessity of calling for them. And by the Fall, after a distressed, and inglorious campaign for want of them, we begin to get a few men, which come in just time enough to eat our Provisions, and consume our Stores without rendering any service; thus it is, one year Rolls over another, and with out some change, we are hastening to our Ruin."

The army ran out of supplies again in the fall of 1780. The future did not look good as it marched into winter

The winter of 1780-81 witnessed the mutiny of the Pennsylvania Continentals.

mutiny: an attempt by soldiers or sailors to overthrow their officers

quarters at camps stretching from West Point, New York, to Morristown, New Jersey.

On January 1, 1781, Pennsylvania Continentals seized several cannons, refused to obey orders, and killed one of their officers. They said that they were going to march to Philadelphia to demand better treatment from Congress. This was a more serious **mutiny** than the one that had involved the Connecticut soldiers. If it spread, the entire army could fall apart. If the Pennsylvania soldiers reached Philadelphia, the government might collapse. Another danger was that the soldiers might go and join the British in New York.

Washington faced a difficult choice. He could either use force against the mutinous soldiers or try to persuade them to stop their illegal actions. Washington decided to allow General Anthony Wayne and some other reliable officers to negotiate with the mutinous soldiers. Meanwhile, the British General Clinton sent a message to the Pennsylvania men. Clinton's messenger promised to welcome them kindly and give them money and food if they joined the British.

The soldiers loyally refused to have anything to do with the British. Then, Pennsylvania politicians met with the mutinous Pennsylvania soldiers. Together they worked out a peaceful end to the mutiny. But on January 20 some New Jersey soldiers mutinied. This time Washington ordered force used against them. Loyal soldiers surrounded the mutinous men and forced them to surrender. Two of the leaders of the mutiny were executed, shot to death by a firing squad made up of twelve soldiers who had loudly supported the mutiny.

Washington knew that the best way to keep the army together was to make the soldiers' lives better. He wrote to the governors of the New England states that "it is vain to think that an Army can be kept together much longer, under such a variety of sufferings as ours has experienced." In spite of Washington's efforts the army suffered through the winter, hungry, naked, and without money to pay the soldiers or to buy food and supplies.

Congress managed to take action. In the past many congressional committees had tried to do the work of caring for the army. The committees had spent much time talking and too little time doing. To make things

Robert Morris patriotically risked his own fortune to help finance the bankrupt government.

French officers cheer General Rochambeau at Newport, Rhode Island.

more efficient, Congress persuaded Robert Morris, a wealthy Philadelphia businessman, to take the post as superintendent of finance. It appointed a good administrator, Colonel Timothy Pickering, to replace Nathanael Greene (who had departed to take command of the rebel army in the south) as the northern army's quartermaster general. Congress did away with the old Board of War and named Benjamin Lincoln to the post of secretary of war.

Robert Morris proved to be the most important change. Morris worked closely with Pickering to get supplies for the army. The old paper money was useless, so Morris began a new system of making contracts with businessmen to provide supplies. Instead of paying with paper money, Morris pledged his own credit, payable in hard currency (gold or silver). This was a temporary, or makeshift, arrangement. An entire nation could hardly run this way. But Morris's credit and the new, more efficient administration could take care of the army for a short period of time. So, Washington's army survived the winter; but as the spring campaign of 1781 began, it was very weak.

More Help from the French

In Newport, Rhode Island, the French General Count Jean Rochambeau believed that time was running out for the American rebels. In May Rochambeau received secret orders from Paris. They told him that a French fleet was to arrive on the American coast sometime in July or August. The orders also told Rochambeau that if the rebel armies fell apart, he was to stop taking orders from Washington and abandon the Americans.

Rochambeau met with Washington to make plans. He asked Washington what the allies should do if a French fleet showed up. Washington wanted to work with the fleet and attack the main British army in New York. Rochambeau did not think it was a good idea. The French general preferred to attack the British in Virginia. Whether the target was New York or Virginia, the two allies had to join forces, so Rochambeau agreed to march his army to join Washington along the Hudson River.

Rochambeau did not tell Washington that a French fleet was sure to appear on the American coast. Instead, Rochambeau wrote to the admiral who commanded the fleet, Count François de Grasse. He said that the American rebels faced a "very grave crisis." Without help from de Grasse the rebels would probably lose the war very soon. There were two places where de Grasse could help: New York and Chesapeake Bay on the Virginia coast. Rochambeau recommended that de Grasse sail to Chesapeake Bay to help attack the British in Virginia.

The summer of 1781 was an anxious time for Washington. He knew that most Americans were tired of a war that just seemed to keep going on without any end in sight. Washington wrote to a discouraged congressman, "we must not despair; the game is yet in our own hands. . . . A cloud may yet pass over us, individuals may be ruined; and the Country at large, or particular States, undergo temporary distress; but certain I am, that it is in our power to bring the War to a happy Conclusion."

On August 14, 1781, Washington learned that Admiral de Grasse was sailing to Chesapeake Bay with his powerful fleet. Washington decided to give up his plans to attack the British in New York and to march to Virginia instead.

CHAPTER TWO

The British in Virginia

The British General Clinton had tried in the past to weaken Virginia by sending forces to raid that state. In 1781 he sent a 1,600-man force commanded by the American traitor, Benedict Arnold, to attack Virginia again.

Washington chose the Marquis de Lafayette to command the small Continental army in Virginia. Cornwallis had no doubt that he could defeat the "boy" general.

In January 1781 Arnold led a destructive raid up the James River all the way to Richmond. Arnold's presence in Virginia proved to be more important than Clinton had anticipated. Arnold was like a "magnet drawing forces of both sides to Virginia."

George Washington ordered the Marquis de Lafayette to march from New York to Virginia with 1,200 Continentals. Washington hoped that Lafayette would be able to trap and destroy Arnold. Washington managed to persuade the French to send a naval force from Newport, Rhode Island, to try to block Arnold's escape by sea. But a British navy force drove the French back to Newport. Clinton sent Major General William Phillips with 2,600 men to join Arnold.

Together, the two generals continued to raid Virginia. Lafayette was too weak to stop the raids. Then the situation got worse for the rebels when General Charles Lord Cornwallis appeared in the state.

After the Battle of Guilford Courthouse, March 15, 1781 (see Volume 9), the British leader, Cornwallis, had retreated to the port of Wilmington, North Carolina. There his battered army received supplies from the Royal Navy. When the American General Nathanael Greene saw that Cornwallis was out of the way, he marched into South Carolina to begin a campaign to reconquer it. Meanwhile, Cornwallis rested his army and considered what to do. He wrote to Major General Phillips, who was in Virginia: "Now my dear friend, what is our plan?...If we mean an offensive war in America, we must abandon New York and bring our whole force into Virginia . . . a successful battle may give us America."

The more Cornwallis thought about strategy, the more he became sure that Virginia was the key. He believed that until the British conquered Virginia, the British hold on the Carolinas would be uncertain. In the middle of April 1781 Cornwallis began marching toward Virginia. He arrived in Petersburg, Virginia, on May 20 and took command of all British forces in Virginia. They numbered some 7,000 men, about one-quarter of the entire British army strength in America.

In response Washington could send only another 800 Continentals commanded by General Anthony Wayne to reinforce Lafayette in Virginia. That left Lafayette too weak to fight Cornwallis. Cornwallis supposedly said of the young Lafayette, "The boy cannot escape me." Cornwallis was wrong. He chased Lafayette, but could not catch his little army. Then Cornwallis received orders from Clinton to march to the coast, build a base, and send part of his force back to New York. Cornwallis marched to Yorktown, a small tobacco port on the York River just within the Chesapeake Bay.

Washington and Rochambeau March to Yorktown

In the past, cooperation between the Americans and the

Opposite Top: Washington chose General William Heath to keep the British bottled up in New York City while Washington himself marched to Virginia.

Opposite Below: Washington issuing orders during the Yorktown campaign

French had been difficult because the different leaders could not get along with each other. When Washington and Rochambeau joined forces, it was different. The two leaders agreed very well with each other. They made a feint, or fake attack, against New York City. Washington left behind only 2,000 Americans to watch Clinton. Then, on August 21, 1781, the allies began a secret march to Virginia.

While Washington was on the march, de Grasse's fleet arrived in Chesapeake Bay. Three thousand French soldiers landed to join Lafayette.

On September 5 the British naval commander in New York, Admiral Thomas Graves, arrived off Chesapeake Bay with 19 ships of the line, the battleships of the age of sail. De Grasse sailed out from the bay with 24 ships of the line to attack Graves. During the Battle of the Virginia Capes (so named because it took place off Cape Henry, Virginia) the French damaged the British fleet,

Continental
soldiers on
the march to
Yorktown

Above: The march from New York to Yorktown took George Washington back to Virginia. He entertained French officers at his Mount Vernon home on September 9-12. It was the first time in six years that Washington had seen Mount Vernon.

Right: The French Admiral de Grasse

but neither side won a clear victory. Yet the battle proved very important because the British fleet had failed to drive off the French. That meant that Cornwallis could neither receive help from the sea nor escape by sea.

For days after the battle the French and British fleets maneuvered to try to gain an advantage. Meanwhile, Admiral Jacques-Melchior Saint-Laurent de Barras had arrived with his force from Newport, Rhode Island. Barras and de Grasse joined forces and presented Graves with too big a force to fight. Graves returned to New York to make repairs. The French fleet now had firm control of Chesapeake Bay. However, de Grasse planned to stay in the area only until October 15.

The Siege of Yorktown

Washington's army reached Yorktown on September 26. After years of trying to concentrate forces for a decisive action, Washington had finally succeeded. He commanded 3,000 Virginia militia and 6,000 Continentals, and was supported by 6,000 French regulars. However, because the French fleet would soon leave, Washington knew that he did not have very much time. But he could not attack Cornwallis's fortifications because they were too strong. Instead, he had to begin a siege.

The French engineers were well trained in siege warfare. They directed both the French and the American forces in the proper way to approach Cornwallis's position. The allies dug trenches and built positions to protect their heavy cannons. Their efforts forced Cornwallis to abandon his forward position on September 30. By October 6 the allies had completed a line of trenches 600 yards from

After the British abandoned their first line at Yorktown, Colonel Alexander Scammell rode ahead to scout. British dragoons surprised and shot Scammell, who later died of his wounds.

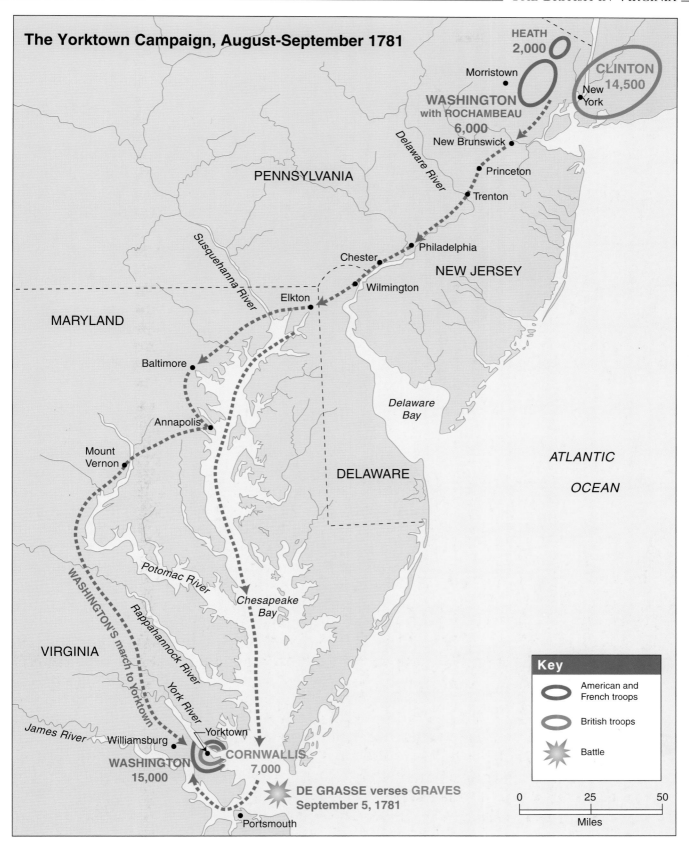

The Yorktown Campaign, August–September 1781

HEATH
2,000

CLINTON
14,500

Morristown

New York

WASHINGTON
with ROCHAMBEAU
6,000

New Brunswick

PENNSYLVANIA

Princeton

Trenton

Delaware River

Philadelphia

Chester

NEW JERSEY

Wilmington

Susquehanna River

Elkton

MARYLAND

Baltimore

Delaware
Bay

Annapolis

Mount
Vernon

ATLANTIC

OCEAN

DELAWARE

Potomac River

Chesapeake
Bay

WASHINGTON'S march to Yorktown

Rappahannock River

VIRGINIA

York River

James River

Williamsburg

Yorktown

WASHINGTON
15,000

CORNWALLIS
7,000

DE GRASSE verses GRAVES
September 5, 1781

Portsmouth

Key

American and
French troops

British troops

Battle

0   25   50
Miles

George Washington fires off the first shot, beginning the allied bombardment at Yorktown.

Cornwallis's main position. The allied artillery opened fire on October 9. The bombardment began to destroy the British fortifications. Next the allies dug trenches toward the British fortifications in order to get closer. By October 11 the allies were only 400 yards away from the British lines.

Two isolated British earthworks, known as Redoubts 9 and 10, kept the allies from getting even closer. Washington ordered a night bayonet attack on October 14 to capture the redoubts. Elite French soldiers led by Lafayette's brother-in-law attacked Redoubt 9. American light infantry-men, commanded by Lafayette and led by Alexander Hamilton, attacked Redoubt 10. The allies competed to see which one would capture a redoubt first. Both allied forces moved forward cautiously with unloaded muskets to prevent any soldier from accidently firing. When they reached the British position, they charged. After a hard 15-minute fight the Americans captured Redoubt 10. A few minutes later the French captured Redoubt 9.

Engineers quickly advanced to rebuild the redoubts so

that the allies could use them. Then the allies dragged their artillery toward the British lines. Cornwallis realized that his best hope was to try to move his men by water across the river to Gloucester Point. The American lines were weak there. Cornwallis hoped that he could attack that weak position and break free. But a storm on the night of October 16 frustrated Cornwallis's plan. The next day he began negotiations on terms of surrender. A little British drummer stood on top of the British fortifications and beat a message on his drum. It was the call to stop fighting. A joyous Pennsylvania soldier wrote that he had "never heard a drum equal to it—the most delightful music to us all." It was exactly four years after Burgoyne's surrender at Saratoga.

Cornwallis had desperately hoped that help would come from New York to save his army. He did not know

Washington inspects the French siege lines. The French and Americans dug trenches and filled sand bags to protect the big guns they used to batter Cornwallis's position.

American soldiers storm Redoubt 10 during a night attack at Yorktown.

that Clinton had been thinking about what to do for days. Finally, on October 17, Admiral Graves sailed from New York with a strong fleet of 25 ships of the line and 7,000 soldiers to help Cornwallis. It was too late.

On October 19, 1781, Cornwallis surrendered. According to legend, when the redcoats marched out of their trenches to surrender, their bands played the tune "The World Turned Upside Down." During the siege Cornwallis's army suffered about 600 casualties. About 8,000 men surrendered. The allies lost only about 400 men during the siege.

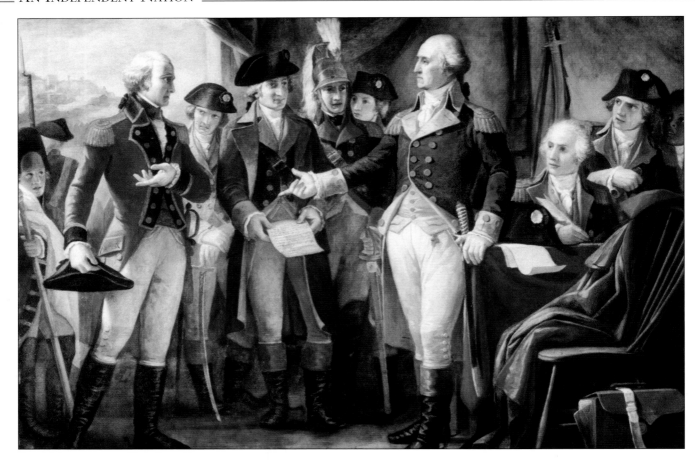

On Sunday, November 25, 1781, a messenger brought the official news about Cornwallis's surrender to Lord Germain's home in London. Germain hurried to tell Lord North. According to Germain, North took the news "as he would have taken a ball in his breast." Over and over North moaned, "O God! It is all over!"

Unlike his ministers, King George refused to admit defeat. Throughout the years leading up to the Revolution and during the war itself King George never changed his mind. He was certain that he was right and so held firm to his goal. The king stubbornly wanted to continue the war. He said, "I trust that neither Lord George Germain nor any member of the Cabinet will suppose that it makes the smallest [change] in those principles of my conduct which have directed me in past time." The king sent a message to Parliament saying that with Parliament's support, "the valour of my fleets and armies," and the "resources of my people," the rebels could still be defeated.

A famous painting in the U.S. Capitol shows Cornwallis surrendering to Washington. In fact, Cornwallis refused to meet with Washington and left his second-in-command, General O'Hara, the unpleasant job of surrendering.

The British army marches out of its defenses to surrender to the allies.

Parliament greeted the king's message with angry questions. Because of the defeat at Yorktown British politicians who had always been against the war grew louder and stronger. Among them was Charles Fox. Fox spoke to the House of Commons and said that all of the nation's troubles came from one source: "The influence of the Crown. To the influence of the Crown we must attribute the loss of the army in Virginia. To the influence of the Crown we must attribute the loss of the thirteen provinces of America; for it was the influence of the Crown in the two Houses of Parliament that enabled His Majesty's ministers to persevere against the voice of reason, the voice of truth, the voice of the people."

Just six months after Yorktown Lord North resigned as prime minister.

Neither War Nor Peace

The surrender at Yorktown ended active campaigning between the American and the British armies. Some

British flags captured at Yorktown are presented to Congress in Philadelphia.

minor fighting still occurred in the south, and fighting against the Indians continued on the frontier. The most brutal fighting took place between Tories and patriots. One incident stood out as a terrible example of the hatred between Americans who had divided over the question of loyalty to the king. During one raid a band of Tories in New Jersey seized Captain Joshua Huddy, a well-known patriot officer. The Tories were angry because one of their leaders, Philip White, had been captured by some rebel militia and then killed, supposedly while trying to escape. The Tories hanged Captain Huddy and left a note pinned to his body. It said, "Up goes Huddy for Philip White."

George Washington protested to British leaders about the atrocity (an atrocity is an act of extreme cruelty). Sir Guy Carleton, who had replaced Clinton in May 1782, said that he very much regretted the hanging even though he had nothing to do with it and promised to try to prevent such things from happening again. His reply did not satisfy Washington. He ordered a British captain executed. Thirteen British prisoners drew straws to see which one would be hanged. A seventeen-year-old captain drew the fatal straw with the label "unfortunate." A hanging match, with first one side and then the other executing a prisoner, would have taken place, except that the French government protested to the Americans. The French protest saved the young British captain.

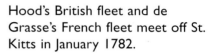

Hood's British fleet and de Grasse's French fleet meet off St. Kitts in January 1782.

After France had allied with the United States, the war had spread all over the world. Although fighting in America ended after Yorktown, it continued in the West Indies, Africa, Europe, and India. In most actions the British gained the advantage. The British won important victories on land and at sea against the French in India. In the West Indies the most important battle took place at sea on April 9–12, 1782, between the islands of Guadeloupe and Dominica. Sir George Rodney's fleet with 37 ships of the line badly defeated de Grasse's fleet with 33 ships of the line. Rodney captured de Grasse and his flagship, the gigantic 110-gun *Ville de Paris* (City of Paris) along with four other French ships.

Overall, the fighting throughout the world did not have much effect on the situation in America. After Yorktown Washington moved his army back to the area of New York to watch the British army that was still in New York. Greene did the same outside of Charleston, and Wayne outside Savannah. The British evacuated Savannah in July 1782. When they left, they took with them 4,000 Tories and 5,000 slaves. In December the British evacuated Charleston. Again about 4,000 Tories left with the British along with thousands more slaves. The last British stronghold on the American coast was

The British fleet under Admiral Sir George Rodney defeats de Grasse at the Battle of the Saints on April 12, 1782.

New York City. Around New York the rebel army commanded by Washington and the remaining British army sat facing one another for a long time while American and British diplomats negotiated a peace.

The Army Disbands

Washington's army served as a piece in a game between American and British diplomats. American diplomats needed the army because it gave force to their demands when they discussed peace terms with British diplomats. If the army fell apart, the American diplomats would have a weaker position. So, while diplomats talked about peace, George Washington struggled to hold his army together.

As had been the case for most of the war, neither Congress nor the army had money to buy the things the army needed to survive. At the time Cornwallis had surrendered at Yorktown, a messenger had ridden to Philadelphia to report the news to Congress. Congress did not even have enough money to pay the messenger. Yet it cost Congress about $20,000 each day to pay for the army's expenses. A North Carolina congressman described how low Congress had sunk. It was "without the means of paying those Debts they Constitutionally

Opposite Top: Although the Americans were only concerned with events in the thirteen states, to Great Britain and its European enemies the Revolutionary War was a conflict fought all over the world. Here the French capture a British fort in Senegal, Africa.

Right: The "Glorious News" of the British surrender at Yorktown appears in Providence, Rhode Island.

GLORIOUS NEWS.

PROVIDĔCE, October 25, 1781.

Three o'Clock, P. M.

THIS MOMENT an EXPRESS arrived at his Honour the Deputy-Governor's, from Col. Christopher Olney, Commandant on Rhode-Island, announcing the important Intelligence of the Surrender of Lord Cornwallis and his Army, an Account of which was printed This Morning at Newport, and is as follows, viz.

Newport, October 25, 1781.

YESTERDAY afternoon arrived in this Harbour Capt. Lovett, of the Schooner Adventure, from York-River, in Chefapeak-Bay (which he left the 20th Inftant) and brought us the glorious News of the Surrender of Lord CORNWALLIS and his Army Prifoners of War to the allied Army, under the Command of our illuftrious General, and the French Fleet, under the Command of his Excellency the Count de GRASSE.

A Ceffation of Arms took Place on Thurfday the 18th Inftant, in Confequence of Propofals from Lord Cornwallis for a Capitulation. His Lordfhip propofed a Ceffation of Twenty-four Hours, but Two only were granted by His Excellency General WASHINGTON. The Articles were completed the fame Day, and the next Day the allied Army took Poffeffion of York-Town.

By this glorious Conqueft, NINE THOUSAND of the Enemy, including Seamen, fell into our Hands, with an immenfe Quantity of Warlike Stores, a forty Gun Ship, a Frigate, an armed Veffel, and about One Hundred Sail of Tranfports.

contracted for the safety of the United States." Congress was "responsible for every thing, and unable to do any thing, hated by the public creditors, insulted by the Soldiery and unsupported by the citizens."

Because the states refused to give Congress the money, officers and men did not receive the pay that was owed them. During the spring of 1782 several Continental Army officers stirred up trouble. At that time Washington had his headquarters in Newburgh, New York. A colonel who said he represented many other officers spoke with Washington. The colonel said that the army was so often in a bad way because Congress failed to take care of it. Washington knew that

One of Washington's staff officers, Colonel Tench Tilghman, announces Cornwallis's surrender at midnight, October 23, 1781, on the steps of Independence Hall in Philadelphia.

was true. The colonel said, "This war must have shown to all, but to military men in particular the weakness of republics." He meant that the problem with republics was that politicians and the people spent too much time talking without ever doing what was needed.

The colonel explained that the army was different. It had proven during the war, and especially at Yorktown, that it could get things done. Officers gave orders, men obeyed. The colonel ended by saying that in order for the United States to work efficiently, he and the other officers wanted Washington to become the king of the United States.

This suggestion was exactly what many rebel politicians had dreaded when Congress created an army back in 1775. From 1775 on, politicians had feared that a strong military man who had the support of the army would take over the government. The study of history had taught many Americans that a regular, or standing, army led to a tyranny, or government rule by force.

Washington replied sternly to the proposal that he should become king: "Be assured Sir, no occurrence in the course of the War, has given me more painful sensations than your information of there being such ideas existing in the Army. . . . If you have any regard for our Country, concern for yourself or posterity [future citizens], or respect for me . . . banish these thoughts." Washington's noble words ended, for the time being, thoughts about making him king.

The winter of 1782–83 again saw the army suffer from hunger and lack of supplies. In mid-March 1783 two papers, called the *Newburgh Addresses,* passed around the army's camp. The *Newburgh Addresses* asked soldiers if, after seven years of hard army service, the country was "willing to redress your wrongs, cherish your worth and reward your services" or was it "a country that tramples upon your rights?" The paper invited officers to a meeting. It suggested that unless the army received proper rewards, the men keep their weapons and resist the government.

Even though the fighting was over, the Continental Army still had a hard time getting food and supplies. A French officer wrote, "It was really painful to see these brave men, almost naked, with only some trousers and little linen jackets, most of them without stockings . . ."

Opposite: Washington and his officers at Newburgh, New York, in 1783.

The *Newburgh Addresses* presented another crisis. Congress had also worried about this kind of thing when it created a standing army. Congressmen knew that throughout history many an unhappy army had marched against its government to make demands.

Washington called for a meeting with his officers. He said that he found the *Newburgh Addresses* shocking. They were an attempt to divide the military from the civilian government. Washington said that he had confidence that Congress would deliver full justice to the army. But, like all civil governments, Congress moved slowly. Washington pledged himself to justice for the army and asked the officers not to tarnish the army's glory by overturning civil rule, or attacking the government. He concluded that if the officers set the example of respect for civil rule, they would be remembered always as good patriots. The officers listened to Washington, and the mutiny against the government ended before it ever really got started.

The Treaty of Paris

After the fall of the North government in Great Britain a new British government led by Lord Shelburne tried to divide the Americans and the French. Shelburne tried to get American diplomats to ignore France and to agree to a **separate peace**. When France first had allied with the American rebels, the Americans had promised never to make a separate peace. That was very important to France because if the United States made a separate peace, France would face the full might of Great Britain. The four American peace commissioners (the men Congress assigned to negotiate a peace), Benjamin Franklin, John Adams, John Jay, and Henry Laurens, kept faith with the French and refused to make a separate peace.

On April 19, 1783, exactly eight years after the first shots at Lexington, an armistice (a special agreement) halted the fighting. A peace agreement ending the war, called the Treaty of Paris, followed on September 3. By its terms Great Britain recognized the independence of the United States. The treaty fixed the republic's

separate peace: an agreement to stop fighting made by only one country out of a group of allies

WASHINGTON'S TRIUMPHAL ENTRY INTO NEW YORK IN 1783

Above Left: A tapestry depicting the Continental Army entering New York City after the British departed on November 25, 1783.

Above: The British army lingered in New York long after the fighting ended. A British army camp, with laundry laid out to dry on top of the tents.

boundaries. Great Britain gave the new nation territory stretching west to the Mississippi River. American fishermen kept the right to use the great fisheries off Newfoundland. The private debts owed by Americans and Britons were supposed to be paid. Congress was supposed to recommend that the states treat the American Tories, or loyalists, fairly. No future action was to be taken against anyone for his role in the war. British forces were to leave American territory "with all convenient speed." All in all, the Treaty of Paris was a very good treaty for the United States.

The British army finally left New York in late November 1783. When the rebels returned to the city, some took revenge against the people who had supported the British. In one typical case patriots seized a Tory, tied him up, cut off his hair, shaved his eyebrows, tarred and feathered his head, and hung a cowbell on his neck with the message:

"Look ye Tory crew
and see what George
your King can do."

After the British army left United States territory, Washington had one last duty. He would show that a nation born by revolution would not be led by a military dictator. Instead, Washington would voluntarily resign from the army and return to civilian life. He traveled to Annapolis, Maryland, to resign formally before

Above: The American flag is raised after the British evacuate New York City.

Congress in December 1783. Congress saw that this was a very important occasion and formed a team of three men to prepare Congress's response. Thomas Jefferson led the three-man writing team.

On December 24 Washington came before Congress. He said, "The great events on which my resignation depended having at length taken place I have now the honor of offering my sincere Congratulations to Congress and of presenting myself before them to surrender into their hands the trust committed to me." He spoke about the devoted officers who had served in his military family from Valley Forge to Yorktown. With great emotion he then handed his commission to the president of Congress.

At that time Washington was the most popular and powerful man in America. Through word and action

Below: George Washington bids farewell to his officers during an emotional dinner on December 4, 1783.

Washington resigns his commission as commander-in-chief on December 23, 1783, in Annapolis, Maryland.

he began a newborn American tradition of civil rule over military rule. Unlike many other nations where a man in a military uniform ran the country, in the United States a civilian would head the government. This historic theme—civilian supremacy over the military—was the subject of Congress's response to Washington. Jefferson had written the words that the president of Congress spoke to Washington: "You have conducted the great military contest with wisdom and fortitude [always] regarding the rights of the civil power through all disasters and changes."

Washington had worked for eight hard years to win independence for the thirteen colonies. Then he left it to civilians to decide what kind of government would control the new nation.

Chapter Three

The New Nation

Political thinkers who lived around the time of the Revolution believed that a republic could only work in special cases. They thought that a republic had to be small and that the people living in it had to share the same race, background, and attitudes.

Europeans knew that the new republic called the United States was very large. It stretched for 1,500 miles from Maine to Georgia. Also, the people living in the United States came from many backgrounds and did not share the same ideas about many things. For those reasons Europeans expected the new nation to fail. A British political thinker said after the Treaty of Paris that the "clashing interests of the Americans, their difference of government, habits, and manners" showed that they could not form and maintain a union. He predicted that Americans would act "suspicious and distrustful of each other" and soon break apart into many separate, smaller countries.

Most Americans expected both their own lives and the fortunes of the United States to improve after peace came. Instead, Americans suddenly found themselves in an unfriendly world. European nations did not want to face economic competition from the United States. So Britain closed its West Indies colonies to American shipping. The West Indian trade was very important to American merchants. The British action was a heavy economic blow. The wartime allies, France and Spain, also took economic action against the United States. France imposed tough controls on important American trade items such as New England fish and Virginia

Opposite: Typical Continental soldiers at the end of the war in the south

tobacco. Spain closed all of its colonies to U.S. trade. Because Spain controlled New Orleans, American settlers west of the Allegheny Mountains could not send their goods down the Mississippi to find a market.

In addition to economic problems the new republic struggled with political problems. Between 1777 and 1787 the United States operated under the Articles of Confederation. The Articles were the country's first constitution. According to the Articles, each state had its own rights. Congress could only ask the states to do things. Congress did not have the power to make states do things. There was no national president. In order to make a change, or amendment, to the Articles, all thirteen states had to agree. That usually proved impossible. In order to make an important decision, nine states had to agree. That often was impossible and always took a long time. During the war Congress's lack of power had made it very difficult for the rebels to fight efficiently. Once peace came, Congress lost even more power.

The Revolutionary War was the biggest influence on the men who were to lead the new nation for the next 25 years. During the war the delegates who served in the Continental Congress shared one belief: The war must be won. That belief acted like glue to unite them. After the war the glue was gone. Different politicians and different states had different visions about which path the republic should follow into the future. The biggest disagreement was about the future role of the federal, or national, government.

On one side was George Washington and many of his officers. Washington had seen his armies suffer terribly. He had seen the different states ignore Congress and fail to send men and supplies to the army. Washington knew that the army had often come close to falling apart. Washington believed that the nation could not work by following the Articles of Confederation. He wanted to make changes so that future leaders would not face the same problems that he had faced. Washington wrote to fellow patriots that now was the time to create an effective federal government. Washington said that there was a choice to create a "respectable and prosperous" republic or a "contemptible and miserable" nation. He added that "the eyes of the whole World" were looking at the United

Like most Anti-Federalists, Virginian Richard Henry Lee chose to stay home rather than attend the Constitutional Convention.

States to see if the experiment to create a new nation would work.

Among the important men who agreed with Washington were Alexander Hamilton, Henry Knox, Timothy Pickering, and James McHenry. Over time their views were taken up by a political party known as the Federalists. The Federalists wanted a strong central government and a standing, or regular, army. They believed that the Continental soldiers had been the military key to winning the war.

On the other side were the Anti-Federalists. The Anti-Federalists were against a strong federal government. They worried that a regular army posed a threat to a nation's liberty. Furthermore, they believed that the nation did not need a standing army because the patriotic militia were enough. The Anti-Federalists believed that the militia had won the war. Over time the Anti-Federalists evolved into a party called the Democratic-Republicans, or Jeffersonians.

Alexander Hamilton

In 1787 delegates traveled to Philadelphia to attend a Constitutional Convention. They met in the same room where the Declaration of Independence had been signed. Thirty of the 55 delegates were veterans from the Revolutionary War. Forty-four, including most importantly John Adams, John Jay, Robert Morris, Gouverneur Morris, and James Madison, had been in Congress during the war. Their common experience had taught them that the Articles of Confederation were too weak. They believed that the nation needed a federal government that could make the states do certain things. The Anti-Federalists did not attend the Constitutional Convention. Men like Patrick Henry, Richard Henry Lee, George Clinton, and Sam Adams stayed home.

Even without the Anti-Federalists there was tremendous debate about how to frame, or build, a new system of government. Slowly the delegates managed to agree on a new system of government, the Constitution. They assigned names and duties to the offices and branches of the national government: President; Congress, with the Senate and House of Representatives; Supreme Court. The framers of the Constitution created a system of checks and balances for the government.

The men who influenced the framing of the Constitution the most were the men who had struggled so long and hard as leaders in the Continental Congress or in the Continental Army. They made sure that the new government had a leader at the top, the president, with strong powers. The central government also had the power "to raise armies and navies," call out the militia (during the Revolutionary War the states controlled the militia), and collect taxes to support itself. When the framers were done, they had created a document that began: "We the People of the United States in order to form a more perfect Union." By the summer of 1788 a majority of the states approved, or ratified the Constitution. The next year the nation elected George Washington to become the first president

Opposite: John Paul Jones, Benjamin Franklin, and George Washington appear at the Constitutional Convention.

Below: Signing the Constitution, September 17, 1787

of the United States. John Adams was his vice-president. As time passed, the Federalist and Anti-Federalist parties gave birth to many more political parties. But their basic quarrel remained the same: Who should have the power to govern, the federal government or the states? It took the Civil War, which began in 1861, to decide the answer.

The New Western Territories

Even while the Revolutionary War was taking place, hundreds of Americans moved west across the Allegheny Mountains to settle on the frontier. In 1770 there were only 200 Americans living in Tennessee and 2,500 in Kentucky. Ten years later the numbers had risen to 2,500 in Tennessee and 7,200 in Kentucky. By 1784 it was clear that the flood of settlers to the west could not be stopped. Kentucky grew so fast that it became a state in 1792, followed by Tennessee in 1796.

Soldiers who had enlisted for the entire war had been promised land on the frontier. The land was a special reward, or bounty. The "soldier's lands" or bounty lands were in Ohio. No official took care to make sure that the soldiers received their land. Instead, many soldiers traded their right to the land to sharp businessmen called land speculators. The land speculators took advantage of the soldiers' ignorance and gave the soldiers only a small amount of money for

Below Left: Settlers descending the Tennessee River aboard a flatboat

Below: Kentucky quickly passed from a handful of struggling settlements to a fully organized state. Here the Kentucky legislature holds its first meeting under the shade of a giant tree.

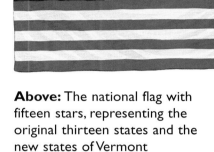

Above: The national flag with fifteen stars, representing the original thirteen states and the new states of Vermont (fourteenth) and Kentucky (fifteenth). Tennessee became the sixteenth state.

Above Left: Settlers in Ohio clear land and build a cabin. Land in Ohio was set aside for army veterans, but few veterans actually moved onto these lands.

valuable land. One victim of the land speculators was a Connecticut soldier who had served loyally for many years. He complained, "When the country had drained the last drop of service it could screw out of the poor soldiers, they were turned adrift like old worn-out horses, and nothing said about land to pasture them upon."

Meanwhile, thousands of hopeful settlers moved west to settle in areas that were the homelands to many Indian tribes. The scene was set for more conflict, and once again the British tried to use the Indians to harm the people of the United States.

Above: The wartime congressman and diplomat, John Jay, was the chairman of a New York group that wanted to end slavery.

How the War Changed the Lives of African Americans

The Declaration of Independence proclaimed that all men had a natural right to claim freedom. Yet the overwhelming majority of the half million blacks who lived in the thirteen states were slaves. Benjamin Rush wrote just before the Revolution, "The plant of liberty is of so tender a nature, than it cannot thrive long in the neighborhood of slavery." But the only group of Americans who were in favor of freeing the slaves during the war were northern Quakers.

Although most Americans supported slavery, most also wanted to end the brutal foreign slave trade. In April

1776 Congress voted to halt the importation, or bringing in, of slaves. By 1787 all the states except South Carolina and Georgia had passed laws prohibiting the slave trade. But those laws did nothing to change the lives of slaves who already lived in the United States.

The ideals connected with documents like the Declaration of Independence caused people to think about whether it was fair for only whites to be free. Slowly, various antislavery groups developed. For example, in 1785, when New York merchants were seizing free blacks and selling them south into slavery, a small group of white leaders formed to end slavery. John Jay was the chairman, and Alexander Hamilton was a member. As the years passed, antislavery groups spread

Slaves pick cotton on a Georgia plantation. Cotton became the south's most valuable product. Cotton farming relied on a tremendous amount of hand labor performed by slaves.

The Revolutionary War showed slave owners that blacks wanted freedom as much as whites. The fear of a slave revolt was a major worry among southern whites. In 1831 Nat Turner led the largest slave rebellion in American history.

the view throughout the north that slavery was wrong. The Northwest Ordinance of 1787, which opened new lands for settlement in the area of modern Ohio, banned slavery from that area.

By 1804 all states north of Maryland and Delaware had passed laws to free, or emancipate, the slaves. As a result, some northern owners freed their slaves. Most sold them to southerners.

Slavery was much more important to the economy of the south than it was to the north's economy. Still, the experience of the Revolution caused changes in the south. Before the war the southern states had laws that made it illegal for owners to free their slaves. In 1782 Virginia repealed the law that prevented owners from freeing their slaves. In 1782 there were about 2,000 free blacks in Virginia. By 1790 that number had increased to 12,866. During the years just after the war southern owners freed more slaves voluntarily than were freed because of new laws in the north. In the whole United States the number of free blacks rose from about 5,000 in 1780 to 60,000 in 1790. The increase in the free black population led to the birth of many new black communities and black social organizations.

The American Revolution caused more Americans to think about how people acted. Such thinking caused many people to conclude that it was wrong to deny any race the basic right of freedom. The only logical way people could argue that blacks did not deserve the same rights as whites was to say that African Americans were born different and inferior. In the years after the war southern slave owners used that argument to justify slavery.

Southern slave owners learned something else from the war. They knew that when British leaders had offered freedom to slaves who escaped from rebel owners, thousands of slaves ran to safety under British protection. So, the war showed that slaves wanted freedom as much as white men. That frightened many slave owners. They concluded that the only way to keep slaves was to treat them more harshly, to watch and guard them to make sure that they did not try to escape to freedom.

The Revolutionary War taught many Americans, mostly in the north, a sense of shame that slavery existed in a free country. They became determined to end slavery. At the same time, most southern slave owners learned that the only way they could keep slaves was to become very stubborn in defense of slavery. Those different lessons from the war made up a huge part of the growing divide between the northern states and the southern states.

Not only did the Revolutionary War change the lives of African Americans, it led to problems that helped drive the United States and Great Britain toward another war in 1812. According to the terms of the Treaty of Paris, the British were supposed to return stolen property to American owners, and Americans were supposed to pay their prewar debts to British merchants. The thousands of slaves who left the southern states to find safety with the British had belonged to southern owners. The slaves were valuable property, and the owners wanted them returned. The British refused, so patriots both seized land that had belonged to the Tories and refused to pay back their debts. Those actions violated the Treaty of Paris.

The British reacted by refusing to turn over to the Americans some of the forts they held on the western frontier. In turn, the British refusal angered the Americans. Both sides believed that the other side had broken the treaty. Anger and suspicion made it more likely that the United States and Great Britain would fight another war.

The Fate of the Native Americans

During the Revolutionary War the British had supported the Indians in their fight against the white Americans.

When the war ended, the great Mohawk chief Thayendanegea, or Joseph Brant to whites, moved his tribe into Canada. He tried and failed to work out a settlement with the United States. More than any other Indian leader, Thayendanegea understood that the only chance the Indians had to resist white settlers was to unite. So, he tried to form a confederation of Indian tribes to defend their land in the upper Ohio Valley and around the Great Lakes. Thayendanegea spent the last years of his life working to improve the lives of his people.

A farmer protects his family from Indians who can be seen among the trees and rocks in the upper right.

The Indians had no idea that King George, the Great White Father across the ocean, would abandon them when the war ended. News of the Treaty of Paris placed the Indians in a weak position because they no longer had the support of Great Britain. The United States struck a first blow in 1783. Congress declared that all Indians who had supported the British had lost all rights to their lands. Congress forced those Indians to sign a new treaty that gave to the United States a large part of modern-day Ohio.

Because of Sullivan's destruction of their homeland back in 1779, the Iroquois tribes who had fought on the British side became homeless refugees. They fled north to Canada, where they could live under British protection. As early as 1779 some 7,365 Indian refugees, including nearly 4,000 Iroquois, had lived in the area around Fort Niagara. When the war ended, the British government settled most Iroquois on a reserve in Canada. During the 1780s the Iroquois had to make treaties giving millions of acres that had once been their homeland to New York and to the United States government.

Among the northern Indians the Oneidas and Tuscaroras had been friendly to the American rebels during the war. Yet they were not rewarded for their service. During the war they lived in "miserable huts" around Schenectady, New York, and barely survived on a meatless diet of potatoes, corn, and squash. Afterward pressure from white settlers forced them to move north and west. Among southern Indians the Catawbas had fought along with the rebels in South Carolina. In 1780 Cornwallis's invasion had forced them to retreat to Virginia. After the war they returned to their South Carolina homes to find their villages ruined and their livestock gone. The state of South Carolina gave the Catawbas only a little bit of help to rebuild their lives.

Whether they fought with or against the rebels, the Indians who had lived in the east were pushed westward by white settlers. Fragments from various tribes tried to find new homes in the territory west of the Allegheny Mountains. But they could not escape from white pressure. The settlers followed them, and that led to a series of Indian wars that continued with great violence for more than 30 years. Before and during the War of 1812 the Indians received support from the British in their fight against the American settlers. From 1783 to 1790 they killed over 1,500 white pioneers. But they could not stop more settlers from moving west.

Henry Knox, who became the head of the U.S. War Department, wrote in 1789 that the Indians who had once lived in the east "have become extinct. If the same causes continue, the same effect will happen, and in a short period the Idea of an Indian on this side [the eastern side] of the Mississippi will only be found in the pages of the historian." Knox accurately predicted the future. By about 1820 the white settlers had killed or driven west over the Mississippi River almost all of the Indians who had taken part in the American Revolution. Only a very few Indians stayed behind to live on small reservations in the eastern states.

In 1811 Governor William Henry Harrison of the Indiana Territory decided to strike the Indians before they raided white settlements in Indiana. The result was the bloody Battle of Tippecanoe fought in November 1811. When war with Great Britain began the next year, the British again used the Indians to fight Americans.

The Fate of the Loyalists

No one knows how many Americans remained loyal to King George III during the war. It was often too risky for loyalists to announce publicly their support for the king. Historians estimate that about one-third of all Americans were loyalists (also called Tories). About 19,000 Tories enlisted in the British army, while another 10,000 served in Tory militias. When loyalists left their homes to enlist with the British army, they had the protection of the rules of war. Local citizens who rose up to support the British by attacking patriot homes and farms did not have such protection. Many savage battles were fought outside of the rules of war between patriots and loyalists, especially in the south.

When the British army controlled an area, the loyalists took revenge against the patriots. When the rebel army controlled an area, the patriots did the same. When the war ended, some loyalists stayed in America. Sometimes they received fair treatment. For example, in Charleston a group of loyalist leaders asked the state government's permission to become full citizens again. Thirty-one got back all of their property and civil rights; 33 got back their property, but were forbidden to hold any public office for seven years; 62 others got their property back, but had to pay a special tax.

But the loyalists could not be sure how they would be treated by the patriots. After all, even reasonable men like George Washington and Benjamin Franklin heartily disliked loyalists. Washington declared that "there never

A British cartoon in 1783 shows "The Cruel Fate of the Loyalists." The Indians are meant to represent Americans. The cartoon criticizes the way the British government abandoned the loyalists to the "savage" American rebels.

existed a more miserable set of Beings than these wretched creatures." Franklin described them as "mongrels" and as people who tried to murder their own family. So, it was not surprising that about 80,000 loyalists left their homes to seek British protection. About half settled overseas, while the rest settled in Florida or parts of Canada. Slave-owning loyalists from the south moved to East Florida, the West Indies, the Bahamas, and Bermuda. There they could continue to live their familiar plantation life. The British government helped support loyalists who fled to England by giving them money. Still, as time passed, many loyalists did not like life in England and left for Canada.

Canada had originally been settled by French-speaking people. So many loyalists moved to Canada that they greatly increased the number of English-speaking people living there. The English speakers changed the way Canada was governed. They also changed Canadian attitudes, making Canada very loyal to Great Britain and opposed to the United States. By 1781, 25,000 loyalists had settled in modern-day Ontario. Ten thousand more loyalists who had lived in New York's Mohawk Valley settled along the St. Lawrence River. When the British evacuated New York in 1783, thousands of loyalists departed for Nova Scotia. By the next year 28,347 loyalists were living in Nova Scotia. They made up more than half of the island's population.

About 50,000 black slaves fled to the British during the war. The British government had promised that slaves who deserted from the rebels would receive their freedom, but only 5,000 actually became free. Many died from disease, were sold back into slavery, or were taken by their loyalist masters to new homes. When the British evacuated New York, 3,360 former slaves were taken to Nova Scotia. There they suffered many hardships. Some English humanitarians worked to find a better place for the black Nova Scotians to live. In 1792 about 1,200 black loyalists sailed from Nova Scotia to Africa, where they founded Freetown, Sierra Leone.

In 1784 Congress asked the states to return property that had once belonged to loyalists. The states refused because, they said, that property made up for the damage the British had done during the war. Several states even passed laws that said if a loyalist returned home, he could be arrested. Over the next three years anger against the loyalists diminished. By 1787 all the states repealed the laws that prevented loyalists from returning. During the next decade thousands of loyalists returned to the United States.

Why the Rebels Won

There were many reasons why the American rebels won the Revolutionary War. George Washington's leadership was one of the main reasons. He had to hold the army together for eight difficult years. The Continental Army

Left: The leadership of George Washington, shown here during the Yorktown campaign, was one of the keys to the rebel victory. One historian described Washington's accomplishment during the war: He "created the Continental Army in the face of obstacles that would have defeated any man of lesser physical and moral stamina."

Above: The inauguration of the first President of the United States, George Washington

indispensable: absolutely necessary

was important not just for military reasons. It was the symbol of the union of the thirteen states. Washington preserved the army. By doing so, he held the states together until the rebels won their independence. Although the behavior of Congress frustrated Washington time and again, he always recognized that Congress, the civil power, had authority over the army, or military power. Washington had to balance military and political needs. Historians call Washington the "**Indispensable** Man" because he was probably the only rebel leader who could have done this so well.

Opposite: The nation relied on the Continental soldiers to win its freedom. Most common soldiers had come from the poorest classes. After the war the state and national governments neglected the Continental veterans, leaving them to return to a life of poverty.

Although Washington was indispensable, many events that led to the American victory took place without his personal influence. Washington had very little influence over four of the war's key battles: Bennington, Saratoga, King's Mountain, and Cowpens.

Any army needs more than just one good leader. Three other American generals showed great military talent during the war: Nathanael Greene, Daniel Morgan, and Benedict Arnold. Those men, along with two foreign volunteers, Baron von Steuben and the Marquis de Lafayette, made key contributions. There were also scores of less famous officers who learned by trial and error how to lead men in battle. As they gained experience, they became very skilled leaders. The Continental soldiers followed them into battle because those officers had earned the soldiers' trust.

The war could not have been won without the dedication of the common Continental soldiers. They repeatedly endured terrible hardships. A list of only some of the more famous events that involved such hardships includes the march to Quebec, the crossing of the Delaware, the winters at Valley Forge and Morristown, and the long marches with very few supplies during Greene's southern campaign. Because they believed in their leaders and in the cause, the Continentals showed more spirit than the British and Hessian professional soldiers.

At important times the American militia also showed great spirit. Because they were civilians, often without training and experience, they broke and ran on many battlefields. But the Continentals needed their help. The willingness of the militia to serve with the army and fight well at such places as Saratoga, Cowpens, and Guilford Courthouse helped shape those battles.

The militia's contribution off the battlefield was perhaps more important. Patriot leaders established firm political control over most of the countryside very early in the war. They used the militia to keep control. The British and Tories learned from hard experience that the only places they controlled were the places where there was a strong British military force. The militia controlled all the other places.

The United States would not have won a clear victory without help from the French. The rebels needed French money and supplies. Almost all of the muskets and

cannons used by the Continental Army came from France. The presence of French forces around the world forced the British to keep forces in many places besides America. But for the French, the British could have sent many more forces to fight the rebels. Last, French control of the sea and French infantry commanded by Rochambeau allowed Washington to win Yorktown.

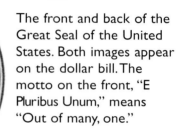

The Revolutionary War created a new nation, the United States, that was unlike any other. Around the time when the framers built the Constitution, delegates also approved the Great Seal of the United States. The words on one side of the seal are in Latin: In English they mean "A new age now begins."

The front and back of the Great Seal of the United States. Both images appear on the dollar bill. The motto on the front, "E Pluribus Unum," means "Out of many, one."

Opposite: Once young Revolutionary War drummers and fifers, now old and plump, lead a patriotic Fourth of July parade.

Below: A Revolutionary War soldier's grave in Charlottesville, Virginia

EPILOG

What Happened to Them?

The Americans and Their Foreign Allies

JOHN ADAMS (see Volumes 1–4, 6, 7, 10): Born in 1735 in Massachusetts, Adams graduated from Harvard and became a lawyer. He married Abigail Smith, who is remembered today for her lively and intelligent letters. After the Revolution John Adams went to Europe to negotiate the peace treaty. He served as vice-president of the United States under George Washington, then became the nation's second president in 1796. His son, John Quincy Adams, became the sixth president of the United States in 1824. John Adams died in 1826.

BENEDICT ARNOLD (see Volumes 2–5, 7, 9, 10): After Arnold's treason was uncovered, the British made him a general in their army and gave a sum of money to him and to members of his family. After the British surrender Arnold moved to England. The government asked his advice on American matters but did not offer him an official position. In 1785 he became a merchant and trader in Canada. Arnold and his family were not liked in Canada, so they returned to England in 1791. His three sons from his first marriage had joined him in Canada, but they returned to America. Arnold was unable to succeed in business and died a poor man in 1801 at the age of 60. His young wife lived only another three years. Arnold's four sons by his second wife, Peggy Shippen Arnold, served in the British army, and one became a general.

BENJAMIN FRANKLIN (see Volumes 1–4, 6, 8, 10): After negotiating the peace treaty in Europe, Franklin returned home and worked on drafting the Constitution. He did not agree with many of its provisions, but he urged people to compromise and show their support for the Constitution. He lived to be 84 years old. He was survived by one daughter. When he died, he was widely mourned in both America and France. Ben Franklin made lasting contributions to the founding of the nation. He also invented the lightning rod, bifocal glasses, and the Franklin stove, all of which are still in use. His *Poor Richard's Almanac* contains many sayings that people still repeat, such as "Never leave that till tomorrow which you can do today."

HORATIO GATES (see Volumes 3–6, 8, 9): Born in England to a servant in 1728, Gates joined the British army as a young man and earned rapid promotions. He fought in the French and Indian War in America, settled in Virginia, and joined the American side in the Revolution. After his defeat at Camden he left the army and asked for an investigation. He was cleared of all blame in 1782 and rejoined the army. After the war Gates retired to his Virginia plantation. Following the death of his first wife, he married a wealthy woman. He freed his slaves in 1790, moved to New York, and spent his wife's fortune helping old soldiers. He lived until 1806.

NATHANAEL GREENE (see Volumes 2, 4, 6, 7, 9, 10): During the Revolution Greene had made bad investments and lost a lot of money. He had to sell his property in Rhode Island to pay his debts. South Carolina and Georgia rewarded him with land for his service in the south, and he settled at an estate, which had been taken from a loyalist, near Savannah in 1785. He died a year later at the age of 44, apparently from sunstroke.

ALEXANDER HAMILTON (see Volumes 4, 6, 10): Hamilton was born in 1757 in the West Indies. He was raised in poverty by his unmarried mother and orphaned at the age of 11. He went to work in a store at the age of 12. Hamilton longed for a college education, and relatives contributed money to send him to New York. He briefly attended college, but quit to form a patriot artillery company in 1775. George Washington selected the intelligent young artilleryman as his aide in 1777. In 1780 Hamilton married a woman from a wealthy family, and they had eight children. Hamilton became frustrated with staff work, quarreled with Washington, and received the combat command he wanted. He bravely led a charge at Yorktown. After the war Hamilton worked as a lawyer and attended the Constitutional Convention. He led the Federalist party and wrote many of the Federalist Papers. He served as secretary of the treasury under President Washington. Historians now believe that Hamilton used his position to meet secretly with the British and unfairly influence foreign relations. He resigned in 1795 and went back to being a lawyer, but took part in politics by campaigning for or against various candidates. Alexander Hamilton fought a duel with Aaron Burr, a politician he had opposed and insulted. He was mortally wounded and died at the age of 47.

PATRICK HENRY (see Volumes 1, 3, 8, 10): After serving as governor of Virginia, Henry retired to a large farm in 1779. He served again as governor from 1784 to 1786. Henry campaigned for the Bill of Rights, the first ten amendments, which were added to the Constitution in 1791. He refused an offer to serve as Washington's secretary of state or chief justice of the Supreme Court and continued to work as a lawyer. Patrick Henry died in 1799 at the age of 63.

HENRY KNOX (see Volumes 3, 4, 6, 7, 10): Henry Knox became a major general and served as commander of West Point in 1782. He became commander-in-chief of the army after Washington resigned. He was the nation's secretary of war from 1785 to 1794. Fort Knox in Kentucky is named after him. Knox was married and had 12 children. He died at the age of 56.

MARQUIS DE LAFAYETTE (see Volumes 6–8, 10): Lafayette's full name was Marie-Joseph-Paul-Yves-Roch-Gilbert du Motier, Marquis de Lafayette. Born in 1757 to a wealthy family in France, he was an orphan by the age of 13. He joined the French army at 13 and married at the age of 16. After victory at Yorktown Lafayette returned to France in 1781. He took part in the French Revolution but had to flee to Austria when a rival party gained power. He returned to France again in 1800 when Napoleon came to power and retired to the countryside. He reentered French politics in 1818, led a force that overthrew the government in 1830, and lived until 1834. Lafayette visited the United States in 1784 at Washington's invitation and again in 1824 at President Monroe's invitation. The American people adored him. He had spent a huge sum of his own money helping the Revolution and had helped convince France to ally with the Americans. A grateful Congress awarded him money, land, and the governorship of Louisiana, which he refused.

Lafayette had one major disagreement with the United States, and with his friend George Washington: He detested slavery. More than a century later, in World War 1, Americans arrived in France to help fight off the German invasion, saying, "Lafayette, we are here." Many places in the United States have been named after Lafayette.

JAMES MADISON (see Volume 10): Born in Virginia in 1851, James Madison helped draft the Virginia state constitution, then served in the Continental Congress during the Revolution. He helped work out compromises so that Americans could form a national government after the war, and he wrote the Bill of Rights. Madison served as the U.S. secretary of state from 1801 to 1809. As president of the United States from 1809 to 1817, Madison led the nation in a second war with Great Britain, the War of 1812.

DANIEL MORGAN (see Volumes 3, 5, 9): Morgan resigned from the army in 1781, after winning the Battle of Cowpens. After the war he commanded militia and was elected to Congress in 1797. He became a wealthy man and owned thousands of acres of land. He died in 1802 at the age of about 65.

THOMAS PAINE (see Volume 4): Thomas Paine continued to write in support of revolution and to contribute what little money he had to the cause. Since he made no money from his valuable writings, Congress gave him a minor job, which he mishandled and had to resign. New York then gave him an estate and a small sum of money, on which he lived until 1787. Paine invented an iron bridge, then went to France and got someone to build it. It was a good design, but as usual, he made no money from it. The French admired Thomas Paine and gave him honorary French citizenship. He lived in France and took part in French politics until 1793, when the government changed, and he was unjustly jailed. While in prison, he began writing a book called *The Age of Reason*. The book made him unpopular because it argued against religion. Washington got him released after a year, and he returned to America. Paine ended his life in poverty. He died in 1809 at the age of 72.

JEAN BAPTISTE DONATIEN DE VIMEUR, COMPTE DE ROCHAMBEAU (see Volumes 9, 10): Born in France in 1725, Rochambeau joined the cavalry at the age of 15 and rapidly rose to command. As part of his long and distinguished military career, he went to America in 1780 as commander of the French army. After the allied victory he returned to France in 1783 and continued a life of military and political service. He was almost beheaded during the French Revolution, but was saved at the last minute. Rochambeau lived until 1807.

FRIEDRICH WILHELM AUGUSTUS VON STEUBEN (see Volumes 6–9): Von Steuben was born in 1730 at an army post in Russia, where his father was serving. He returned to Germany for his education and joined the army as a teenager. He left the army as a captain in 1763 and held a position in the palace of a minor prince. He fell into debt and offered his services to the Americans because he needed a job. He agreed to start work as a volunteer and arrived in America in 1778. He was so good at training the Continentals at Valley Forge that he won rapid promotion to major general. After the war von Steuben helped Washington plan for the future of the army. He became an American citizen and settled in New York on land given to him by the state. His free-spending habits plunged him back into debt, and Congress gave him a sum of money. A lifelong bachelor, von Steuben died in 1794.

GEORGE WASHINGTON: The delegates to the Constitutional Convention in 1787 insisted that George Washington serve as their presiding officer. Washington became the nation's first president in 1789. He was elected to a second term, but refused a third term in 1796. He briefly interrupted his retirement in 1798 to serve as commander-in-chief of a provisional army organized when it appeared the nation might have another war. Washington died at Mount Vernon in 1799 at the age of 67. His wife Martha, whom Washington had married in 1759 when she was a widow with two children, lived until 1802. Their marriage produced no children, but Washington was very fond of his stepchildren. When his stepson died leaving four children, Washington adopted two of them. Numerous places, including a state and the nation's capital, are named after George Washington. As president, Washington laid the cornerstone for the Capitol building in 1793. The national government remained in Philadelphia until the government buildings in Washington, D.C., were completed in 1800.

The British

JOHN BURGOYNE (see Volumes 2–6): After his defeat at Saratoga Burgoyne got permission from the Americans to return to England. He was anxious to give his side of the story and argue that he was not to blame for the British defeat. The official investigation did not clear Burgoyne's name, so he became bitter and resigned from his high position in the army. He published his arguments, shifting blame for the defeat from himself to others. After the British surrender at Yorktown Burgoyne was made commander-in-chief of the army in Ireland. He retired from public life in 1784, wrote several successful plays, and died 10 years later at the age of 70. One of his sons served with the British army in America during the war of 1812.

HENRY CLINTON (see Volumes 2–5, 7–10): Clinton got most of the blame for the British loss of America. He was forced to retire from the army. Clinton won election to Parliament in 1790, became governor of Gibraltar in 1793, and died there in 1795 at age 65. Two of his sons became generals in the British army.

CHARLES CORNWALLIS (see Volumes 4–10): In spite of his defeat, Cornwallis was well thought of among the most powerful people in England, particularly since Henry Clinton received most of the blame for losing the war. Cornwallis served as governor-general of India from 1786 to 1793 and viceroy (royal governor) of Ireland from 1798 to 1801. He was again appointed to serve as governor-general of India in 1805, but he died shortly after his arrival there, at age 66. Cornwallis made important reforms to the colonial governments. His insistence on honorable behavior by British colonial officials improved the worldwide reputation of the British government.

RICHARD HOWE (see Volumes 4, 6, 7): Admiral Richard Howe had first gone to sea at the age of 14. He resigned and returned to England in 1778. He returned to active naval service in Europe in 1782 and served as the First Lord of the Admiralty from 1783 to 1788. In 1794, when he was nearly 70 years old, he took active naval command in a war with France and performed brilliantly. He died in 1799.

WILLIAM HOWE (see Volumes 2–7): William Howe had been a soldier since the age of 17. When he resigned his command and returned to England in 1778, many blamed him for British defeats in America. He lost his seat in Parliament, which he had held for 20 years. Howe did not believe he was to blame. The king still liked Howe, so Howe remained in active army service until 1803. He lived to be 85 years old.

KING GEORGE III (see Volumes 1–5, 7–10): George III finally admitted defeat and accepted the United States as an independent nation. He remained in power as king until 1811, when he went insane after the death of his favorite daughter. His son served in his place until George III's death in 1820 at the age of 81, at which time the son was crowned King George IV.

BANASTRE TARLETON (see Volumes 8, 9): Banastre Tarleton was born to a wealthy merchant's family and received a university education before he joined the British army. After the Revolution he published a book about his battles in America, served in Parliament, held several military commands, was promoted to general in 1812, and knighted in 1820. He married but had no children. He died in 1833.

Army and Navy Ranks in the American Revolution

During the American Revolution the newly formed Continental army and navy used the same ranks as the British army. Until they started fighting the British, some American soldiers and sailors had been serving in the British military forces, and they organized their new forces according to what they knew. The ranks are listed from lowest to highest.

Army

Private: the lowest rank at which a common soldier enlisted in the army

Corporal: the lowest noncommissioned (not appointed) officer rank

Sergeant: the rank above corporal. Sergeants were the vital link between the officers and the common soldiers.

Ensign: the lowest officer rank. Ensigns carried the regimental flag, also called an ensign. They often entered the army as young teenagers.

Lieutenant: second in command of a company

Captain: officer in command of a company

Major: commander of a group of companies and assistant to the colonel

Lieutenant colonel: the second in command of a regiment; called "colonel" in conversation

Colonel: the commander of a regiment

Brigadier general: the commander of a brigade. All three ranks of general were called "general" in conversation.

Major general: the commander of a division

Lieutenant general: the highest rank for generals at the time of the Revolutionary War. George Washington was the first American to hold this rank. In the next 100 years only Winfield Scott and Ulysses S. Grant held this high rank.

Navy

Landsman: a sailor with no sailing experience

Ordinary Seaman: a sailor with some experience at sea

Able Seaman: a sailor who had mastered the tools of his trade

Midshipman: the lowest rank for an officer. Most midshipmen were teenagers, some as young as thirteen years of age.

Lieutenant: second in command to a commander or captain

Commander: a commanding officer of an unrated, or small, ship

Captain: commanding officer of a rated ship. All commanders of ships were called "captain" in conversation, but only a true captain could be promoted to commodore or rear-admiral.

Commodore: a captain temporarily placed in charge of a squadron of ships

Rear-admiral: the lowest grade of admiral, in command of the rear ships in a squadron. A captain could be promoted directly to rear-admiral because commodore was only a temporary rank.

Admiral: the highest rank for a naval officer

Chronology

January 1, 1781: Pennsylvania Continentals mutiny.

January 20, 1781: New Jersey Continentals mutiny.

January 1781: The American traitor Benedict Arnold leads raids against Americans in Virginia.

May 20, 1781: General Cornwallis arrives in Virginia and takes command of the British troops.

August 14, 1781: Washington learns that the French fleet is on the way to the Virginia coast and decides to march his army to meet it.

August 21, 1781: Washington's Continental Army and Rochambeau's French force secretly begin their march to Virginia.

September 5, 1781: De Grasse's French fleet holds off a British fleet in the Battle of the Virginia Capes, cutting off Cornwallis from naval help.

September 26, 1781: Washington's and Rochambeau's armies reach Yorktown, Virginia. With 15,000 men they begin a siege of Cornwallis's 8,000-man British army.

October 9, 1781: American and French artillery begin firing on Yorktown.

October 19, 1781: Cornwallis surrenders his British army to the allies.

July 11, 1782: The British evacuate Savannah, Georgia, taking with them 4,000 loyalists and 5,000 slaves.

December 1782: The British evacuate Charleston, South Carolina.

September 3, 1783: The Treaty of Paris is signed by England, France, and the United States.

Glossary

AGE OF SAIL: the period of history before engines were invented, when ships used sails to move across the water

ALLIES: nations that are fighting on the same side in a war; used here to mean the nations fighting against the British during the American Revolution

AMENDMENT: a statement added to a governing document that changes its original meaning

ARMISTICE: a truce during the period before a formal peace treaty is signed

ARTICLES: statements that make up a governing document

ARTILLERY: a group of cannons and other large guns used to help an army by firing at enemy troops

CONFEDERATION: a group of governments that agree to a long-term union

DELEGATES: representatives sent to a congress, meeting, or convention

EARTHWORKS: walls made of dirt to protect soldiers on a battlefield

FEDERAL: related to the central government of the United States

FORTIFICATIONS: defensive structures, such as walls and forts, equipped with weapons

INDISPENSABLE: absolutely necessary

LINES: battle formations consisting of lines of soldiers, weapons, and defenses

MILITIA: a group of citizens not normally part of the army that mobilizes for the purpose of defending the homeland in an emergency; also used as a plural to describe several such groups

MUTINY: an attempt by soldiers or sailors to overthrow their officers

QUAKER: member of a Christian religious group called the Society of Friends (founded in England around 1650) that favors simple ways and opposes war

REDOUBT: a temporary stronghold or fortification often built in front of the main position

REPUBLIC: a nation ruled by voters and their elected officials

SEPARATE PEACE: an agreement to stop fighting made by only one country out of a group of allies

SHIP OF THE LINE: a warship large enough to be part of a line of battle

SIEGE: a campaign to capture a place by surrounding it, cutting it off from supplies, and attacking it cautiously by advancing under the cover of trenches and earthworks

STANDING ARMY: an army that is kept ready for war even in times of peace, made up of full-time professional soldiers

TORIES: American colonists who sided with England during the American Revolution; also called loyalists

TRENCHES: ditches dug on a battlefield as a place for soldiers to take cover

TYRANNY: government by a ruler with absolute power

Further Resources

Books:

Faber, Doris and Harold Faber. *The Birth of a Nation: The Early Years of the United States.* New York: Charles Scribner's Sons, 1989.

Ferrie, Richard. *The World Turned Upside Down: George Washington and the Battle of Yorktown.* New York: Holiday House, 1999.

Fleming, Thomas. *First in Their Hearts: A Biography of George Washington.* Lakeville, CT: Grey Castle Press, 1984.

Marrin, Albert. *George Washington and the Founding of a Nation.* New York: Dutton, 2001.

Murphy, Jim. *A Young Patriot: The American Revolution as Experienced by One Boy.* New York: Clarion Books, 1996. Based on the life story of a real person, Joseph Plumb Martin, who was 15 years old when he enlisted in the Continental Army.

Smith, Carter, ed. *The Founding Presidents: A Sourcebook on the U.S. Presidency.* Brookfield, CT: Millbrook Press, 1993.

Young, Robert. *The Real Patriots of the American Revolution.* Parsippany, NJ: Silver Burdett, 1996.

Websites:

http://library.thinkquest.org/10966/
The Revolutionary War—A Journey Towards Freedom

ushistory.org/march/index.html
Virtual Marching Tour of the American Revolution

http://www.pbs.org/ktca/liberty/chronicle/index.html
Chronicle of the Revolution
Read virtual newspapers of the Revolutionary era

Places to Visit:

Independence National Historical Park, Philadelphia, Pennsylvania
The U.S. Constitution was signed at Independence Hall, part of the park.

Mount Vernon, Alexandria, Virginia
George Washington's estate and burial place

Yorktown Battlefield, Colonial National Historical Park, Williamsburg, Virginia

About the Authors

James R. Arnold has written more than 20 books on military history topics and contributed to many others. Roberta Wiener has coauthored several books with Mr. Arnold and edited numerous educational books, including a children's encyclopedia. They live and farm in Virginia.

Set Index

Bold numbers refer to volumes; *italics* refer to illustrations

Acland, John **5:** 60–61
Acland, Lady Harriet **5:** *61*
Adams, Abigail **10:** 60
Adams, John **1:** 44, 56, 60; **2:** 46, 51–52; **3:** 60, 62; **4:** 16, 29–30, 44; **6:** 21, 29, 43; **7:** 13, 15; **10:** 31, 39, *60*
Adams, John Quincy **10:** 60
Adams, Samuel **1:** 41, 44, 51–53, 57–58; **2:** 7, 19, 24–25, 51; **3:** 60; **6:** 43
Africa **10:** 25–27, 53
African Americans **2:** 53; **3:** 48, 64; **4:** 55; **7:** 36–37, 66; **10:** 44–47
   Armistead, James **7:** 36
   Lee, William **7:** 36
   Poor, Salem **7:** 36
   Slaves **7:** 36–37, 63; **8:** 50, 64; **10:** 25, 44, 46–47, 53
   Turner, Nat **10:** 46
   Whipple, Prince **4:** 55
Alexander, William (Lord Stirling) **4:** *24*, 27; **7:** 47, 55
Allegheny Mountains **1:** 21, 22, 37, 55; **10:** 38, 42, 50
Allen, Ethan **1:** 31; **2:** 47, 50–*51*; **3:** 28–29
André, John **6:** 31; **7:** 41; **9:** 12–15
Armistead, James **7:** 36
Armstrong, John **6:** 24
Army organization **3:** 16–19
   Infantry **3:** 16–19
Army, standing **4:** 44–45; **10:** 28, 31, 39
Arnold, Benedict **1:** 31; **2:** 50; **3:** 26, 30–35; **4:** 15–19, 21, 66; **5:** 26, 44–45, 48, 51, 53, 55, 58, 60–63; **7:** 48; **9:** 10–15; **10:** 11, 57, *60*
Arnold, Peggy (Shippen) **7:** *48*; **10:** 60
Articles of Confederation **10:** 38–39
Artillery; see also Weapons **1:** 25; **3:** 22–23, *38–41*; **4:** 26, 56; **5:** 29, 60, 63; **6:** 28, 41; **7:** 55; **9:** 50, 54–55; **10:** 18–19
Attucks, Crispus **1:** 45

Balfour, Nisbet **9:** 64
Bancroft, Edward **5:** 13
Barras, Jacques **10:** 15

Battle formation **2:** 49; **8:** 64; **9:** 34
Baum, Friedrich **5:** 33–36
Bayonets; see Weapons
Bemis Heights (N.Y.), battle **5:** 58–63
Bennington (Vt.), battle **5:** 33–39, 45–46, 48
Blacks; see African Americans
Blockades **3:** 64; **4:** 13–14, 21, 65–66; **6:** 66
Bonhomme Richard vs. *Serapis* **7:** 23–31
Boone, Daniel **8:** 8, 11
Boston Massacre **1:** *43–47*; **3:** 37
Boston (Mass.), siege **3:** 36–45; **7:** 11
Boston Tea Party **1:** 51, *52–53*, 54–55, 57; **2:** 16, 18
Boycotts **1:** 42, 44–45, 57
Boyd, James **7:** 67
Braddock, Edward **1:** 19, 24–25, *28*
Brandywine (Pa.), battle **6:** 18, 22–28, 36; **7:** 56
Brant, Joseph **5:** 41; **8:** *21–22*; **10:** 48
Breymann, Heinrich **5:** 35–36, 62–63
Breed's Hill; see Bunker Hill
British armed forces **1:** 24–26, 28, 31, 34–35, *36–37*, 42–43, 62–63; **2:** 6–7, *17–18*, 43, 49, 55; **3:** 8, 14; **4:** 11; **6:** 8; **7:** 40; **8:** 46, 65; **9:** 38; **10:** 25, 32–33, 51, 57
   African Americans **7:** 37
   Dragoons **4:** 49; **9:** 35–36, 38–39
   Grenadiers **2:** *19*, 22, 36–37, 61, 63; **3:** 49; **6:** *25*; **7:** 55
   Light infantry **2:** 12, 22, 28, 36–37, 63; **4:** 34; **6:** 38; **7:** 55, 66
   Scottish Highlanders **3:** 9, *50–52*; **4:** 34, *36*; **9:** 36, 39, 42
   Strength **3:** 28, 31, 44, 46, 51; **4:** 11–12, 14–15, 38–39, 43, 48; **5:** 39–40, 45, 48, 50–51, 56, 58; **6:** 12, 24, 36; **7:** 40–41, 60, 65; **8:** 29, 34, 46, 49; **9:** 30–31, 36, 58, 65; **10:** 12, 21
British Empire **1:** 14–16, 46, 49; **5:** 7; **7:** 62
British government **1:** 14–16; **3:** 6–7; **4:** 10–12; **5:** 6, 8; **7:** 6, 8; **8:** 6
British laws
   Boston Port Act **1:** 54, 57; **2:** 12, 19
   Declaratory Act **1:** 42
   Intolerable Acts **1:** 56, 59, 60
   Quartering Act **1:** 43, 55; **2:** 13
   Quebec Act **1:** 55–56
   Stamp Act **1:** 39–42
   Sugar Act **1:** 37–38

Tea Act **1:** 50

Townsend Revenue Act **1:** 42, 45

Brown, Thaddeus **2:** 27

Brown, Thomas **8:** 61; **9:** 63–64

Buford, Abraham **8:** 54, 64

Bunker Hill (Mass.), battle **2:** 53–66; **3:** 6–7, 13, 38; **4:** 38; **5:** 29

Burgoyne, John **2:** 55, 65; **3:** 10; **4:** 15; **5:** 8–11, 14–16, 18–21, 23–33, 39–40, 43, 45–48, 50, 54–58, 60, *63–65*; **6:** *16*–17, 43, 63, 66; **7:** 68; **10:** 19, *66*

Burr, Aaron **3:** 34; **4:** 33–34; **10:** 62

Burke, Edmund **1:** 46–47; **3:** 8–9

Butler, John **8:** 18–19

Butler, Walter **8:** 19, 22

Cadwalader, John **4:** 52–53, 59, 66; **7:** *50*

Camden (S.C.), battle **8:** 56–60, 65, 67; **9:** 10, 16–17, 26, 32, 38, 47

Campbell, Archibald **7:** 65–67; **8:** 27

Campbell, William **9:** 47

Canada **1:** 20–21, 29, 34–35, 36, 55–56; **4:** 14–17; **5:** 7–10, 12, 14, 18, 29, 46, 56; **6:** 9, 16; **8:** 6, 18–19; **10:** 49–50, 53

    Halifax **3:** 45; **4:** 6, 22; **8:** 40

    Invasion of **3:** 23–35; **4:** 15–17; **10:** 57

    Louisbourg **1:** 18, *34–35*; **3:** *24–25*

    Montreal **3:** 26, 29; **4:** 15

    Quebec **1:** 20, 35; **3:** 26, 29–35; **4:** 15

    St. Johns **3:** 28–29; **4:** 17

Cannons; see Weapons

Carleton, Guy **3:** 24, 28; **4:** 15, 17–18, 20; **5:** 7–8, 14, 18, 46; **10:** 24–25

Casualties **1:** 26, 28; **2:** 34–35, 44, 66; **3:** 35, 44, 49, 52, 59; **4:** 29, 35, 43, 56, 62; **5:** 36, 54, 63; **6:** 28, 31, 40, 42; **7:** 31, 56, 66–67; **8:** 25, 28, 31, 38–39, 42, 53, 59, 64; **9:** 24, 42, 49, 56–57, 62, 64–65, 68; **10:** 21

Caswell, Richard **2:** 51

Cavalry **3:** 20–22; **5:** 33; **6:** 24–25; **8:** 52, 54, 64; **9:** 35, 40–41, 46, 54

Champe, John **9:** 15

Charleston (S.C.), siege **8:** 48–54

Chesapeake Bay **4:** 13; **6:** 19; **7:** 16; **10:** 10, 12–13, 15

Church, Benjamin **2:** 12, 18

Cincinnatus **2:** 44–45

Clark, George Rogers **8:** 11–16

Clinton, George **10:** 39

Clinton, Henry **2:** 55, 63, 66; **3:** 10–11, *54–55*, 59; **4:** 48; **5:** 55–58; **7:** 40–41, 43–44, 47–52, 55–56, 65; **8:** 34–37, 48–54, 61; **9:** 11, 14, 24, 31, 44, *65*; **10:** 6, 8, 10, 12–13, 21, 24, *66*

Clinton, James **8:** *24–25*

Clymer, George **3:** 60

Colonies, life in **1:** 8–16

Committees of Correspondence **1:** 44, 53, 57

Communication: **4:** 10; **5:** 9–10, 56; **6:** 16

Concord (Mass.), battle **2:** 16, 18–19, 21, 28–44

Congress, United States **10:** *24*, 26–28, 31–32, 34–35, 38, 45, 49

Connecticut **2:** 6–7, 50; **6:** 13; **8:** 65–66; **10:** 6

Constitution, United States **10:** 39–40, 58, 61

Continental Army **2:** 51–52; **3:** *11–12*, 13, 36, 63–66; **4:** 44–45; **6:** 24–25, 46–50, 52–56; **7:** 36, 45, 47; **8:** 19, 25, 42, 47, 52; **9:** 34–35, 37, 39, 50, 58–60; **10:** 6–8, *14*, 26, *30*, 32, *37*, 40, 54, 57

    Dragoons **9:** 29, 35

    Light infantry **5:** 51, 61; **6:** 25; **8:** 37; **10:** 18

    Ranks/Officers **3:** 12–16; **6:** 14; **10:** 34, 68

    Strength **3:** 13, 25–26, 31, 36, 40; **4:** 15, 22, 31, 38–39, 42–43, 47, 52, 58; **5:** 11, 21, 31, 40, 44, 58, 64; **6:** 11, 24, 36; **7:** 47, 60, 66–67; **8:** 24, 28, 30, 47, 51, 57, 65; **9:** 27, 30, 35, 47, 58, 65; **10:** 12–13, 16

Continental Congress

    First **1:** 6–7, 58–60

    Second **2:** 46–47, 51–52; **3:** 11–13, 24, 36, 40, 55, 62, 65–66; **4:** 15, 22, 29–30, 32, 44–46, 49–50; **5:** 11, 13, 17–18, 28, 38, 45, 65, 67; **6:** 8, 10, 14–16, 20–21, 29, 34–35, 42–44, 51–52, 61, 66–67; **7:** 13, 15–16, 18, 20, 31, 47, 59, 61, 66; **8:** 17, 23, 40, 55, 65–67; **9:** 10, 26–27; **10:** 8–9, 38, 40, 55

Continental Marines **3:** 13; **6:** 37; **7:** 15–16, 24, 30; **8:** 40

Continental Navy **7:** 11–20, 32, 36; **8:** 40

    Ranks **10:** 68

Conway Cabal **6:** 42–44, 52

Conway, Thomas **6:** 43–44

Cornwallis, Charles **4:** 48–50, 58–59, 61; **5:** 9; **6:** 9, 23, 25, 27, 35, 58; **7:** 44, 52; **8:** 48–49, *54–56*, 59; **9:** 16, *18*, 24–25, 27–31, 42, 44–52, 54, 56–58; **10:** 12, 15–16, 18–19, 22,

26, 28, 66
Cowpens (S.C.), battle   9: 32–44, 46; 10: 57
Cruger, John   9: 64
Cunningham, Patrick   3: 53
Currency, Continental   3: 65–66; 6: 14, 50;
    8: 42–43, 47, 67; 9: 10; 10: 9

Davie, William   8: 62; 9: 60
Davis, Isaac   2: 32, 34
Dawes, William   2: 24–25, 28
Deane, Silas   5: 13; 6: 20, 61
Dearborn, Henry   2: 58; 5: 51, 61; 8: 24
Declaration of Independence   1: 7; 3: 60–63;
    7: 40; 10: 39, 44–45
Delaplace, William   2: 50–51
Delaware   1: 19; 2: 6; 6: 17, 19, 34, 53
Delaware River   4: 28, 49–50, 53–58; 6: 17, 19,
    35–36, 41–43; 7: 43–44, 48; 10: 57
Desertion   3: 32; 4: 15; 5: 31, 58; 6: 33; 7: 9;
    8: 65; 9: 47, 56, 65, 67–68
Disease   3: 35, 40; 4: 15–16, 22, 41; 6: 33, 49;
    7: 9, 38, 65; 8: 17, 29–30, 57, 67; 9: 49, 63
Drill; see Training, military
Duportail, Louis   6: 17

East India Company   1: 50, 53
England   1: 46–47, 53, 57; 3: 9; 4: 44, 51;
    5: 11–13; 6: 62–63, 66; 7: 21–23, 32–33, 35,
    38–39; 8: 6, 31–33, 50; 9: 57; 10: 31–32, 36,
    43, 47–48, 53
d'Estaing, Charles   7: 39, 47, 58–61, 68;
    8: 28–31; 9: 6
Europe   1: 8, 14, 24–25, 35, 37; 3: 19; 6: 35;
    7: 21, 31; 10: 25, 36
Eutaw Springs (S.C.), battle   9: 65–68

Fanning, David   9: 64
Farm, Matthias   5: 22
Farnsworth, Amos   2: 65
Ferguson, Patrick   9: 18–25
Flag, United States   6: 10, 22; 10: 43
Fletchall, Thomas   3: 53
Florida   7: 65–66; 8: 31–32; 10: 53
Fort Anne   5: 23–24
Fort Duquesne   1: 22, 24
Fort Edward   5: 28–29
Fort Granby   9: 63
Fort Johnson   3: 55; 8: 50, 52

Fort Johnston   3: 49–50
Fort Lee   4: 42–43, 47
Fort Mercer   6: 41–42
Fort Mifflin   6: 41–42
Fort Motte   9: 63
Fort Moultrie   3: 55–59; 7: 63; 8: 31, 50, 52–53
Fort Necessity   1: 22–23, 24
Fort Sackville   8: 15–16
Fort Stanwix   5: 11, 14, 40–45; 6: 9
Fort Ticonderoga   1: 34; 2: 7, 50–51; 3: 23–24,
    28, 38; 4: 16–17, 20; 5: 11, 14, 16, 20–22,
    24–25, 30, 45–46, 55; 6: 9, 16
Fort Washington   4: 38, 40, 42–43, 47
Fort Watson   9: 59
Fort William and Mary   2: 10–11
Fox, Charles   3: 8–9; 10: 23
France   4: 63; 5: 1–13, 65; 6: 41, 60–67; 7: 8,
    20, 23, 32–33, 35, 38–39, 59; 8: 6, 31, 55,
    67; 9: 10; 10: 25, 31, 36, 57–58, 61, 63–64
Francisco, Peter   9: 56
Franklin, Benjamin   1: 16, 28, 36, 39, 41, 53;
    2: 46, 50; 3: 60, 62; 4: 29–30, 51; 6: 61–66;
    7: 26; 8: 32; 10: 31, 41, 52–53, 61
Fraser, Simon   5: 24–25, 50, 53, 55, 61–63
Freeman's Farm (Saratoga), battle   5: 50–55, 58
French alliance   6: 41, 60–67; 7: 32, 41, 47, 61,
    68; 8: 13, 32; 9: 6
French and Indian War   1: 17–37; 2: 7, 11, 51,
    59; 3: 24; 5: 2, 17; 8: 6
French armed forces   1: 22–26, 31, 34–35;
    8: 29–31; 9: 6, 9; 10: 13, 16, 19, 58
    Engineers   10: 16, 19
French fleet   7: 33–34, 38–39, 47, 59–60;
    8: 28–29, 32; 9: 6, 10; 10: 10–11, 13, 15–16,
    25
Frontier   1: 29; 8: 6–7; 9: 19; 10: 42, 48, 50

Gage, Thomas   1: 28–29, 40, 54, 61–63;
    2: 10–12, 18–19, 21–22, 26, 44–45, 50,
    55–57; 3: 10–11, 37
Galloway, Joseph   6: 60; 7: 44
Gansevoort, Peter   5: 40
Gaspee incident   1: 47–49
Gates, Horatio   1: 29; 3: 12, 15; 4: 16, 18, 52;
    5: 45, 48, 50–51, 53, 55, 58, 60, 64; 6: 43;
    8: 55, 57, 59–60, 65, 67; 9: 10, 16, 26; 10: 61
George II, King   1: 16, 22; 3: 50
George III, King   1: 16, 41, 42, 45, 46, 48, 55,

60–63; **2:** 11, 44, 52; **3:** 6, 9; **4:** 12, 29, 63; **5:** 6–7, 14, 25; **7:** 62, 68; **8:** 32, 61; **9:** 57; **10:** 22–23, 49, *67*

Georgia **1:** 12, 58, 60; **7:** 43, 65–68; **8:** 27–29, 36, 55–56, 61, 65; **9:** 16, 30, 44, 58, 63; **10:** 45, 61

    Savannah **1:** 12; **7:** 65–66; **8:** 27, 29–31, 48, 56, 61; **9:** 6, 68; **10:** 25

Germain, George **3:** 6–8, 37; **4:** 10, 14; **5:** 6–8, 11, 14; **7:** 41; **8:** 48; **9:** 31; **10:** 22

German Battalion **4:** 52, 58

Germantown (Pa.), battle **6:** 36–41, 63

Girty, Simon **8:** 11, 16

Glover, John **4:** 28, 38, 53, 66

Government, United States **10:** 38–40

    Political parties **10:** 39, 42

de Grasse, Francois **8:** 29; **10:** 10, 13, *15*, 25

Graves, Thomas **10:** 13, 15, 21

Great Bridge (Va.), battle **3:** 49

Great Britain; see British; also see England

Green Mountain Boys **2:** 50–51; **3:** 28; **5:** 24

Greene, Christopher **7:** 36

Greene, Nathanael **2:** 54; **4:** 24, 31–32, 43; **6:** 20–21, *24*, 28, 52; **7:** 50, 55.59; **8:** 47, 55; **9:** 25–32, 44, 46–47, 49–52, 55–60, 62–65, 67–68; **10:** 9, 12, 25, 57, *61*

Grey, Charles **6:** 31–32

Grierson, Benjamin **9:** 63

Guerillas; see also Partisans **4:** 8; **8:** 62; **9:** 16, 29, 35

Guilford Courthouse (N.C.), battle **9:** 49–58, 62; **10:** 12, 57

Hale, Nathan **4:** 40; **9:** 15

Hamilton, Alexander **4:** 56, 61, 66; **6:** 53; **8:** 59; **10:** 18, 39, 45, *62*

Hamilton, Henry **8:** 9, 14–15

Hancock, John **2:** 6–7, 19, 24–25, 46; **3:** 60

Hand, Edward **4:** 58, 66; **8:** 23

Harlem Heights (N.Y.), battle **4:** 32, *34–35, 36*, 38

Hart, Nancy **8:** 64

Hausegger, Nicholas **4:** 52, 58

Heath, William **4:** 42; **10:** 13

Henry, Patrick **1:** *38–39*, 40, 44, 59; **3:** 11, *46–48*; **8:** 11, 14; **10:** 39, *62*

Herkimer, Nicholas **5:** 41–*42*

Hessians **4:** 12–15, 48–49, 52, 53, 55–57, 63;

5: *11*, 14, 20, 23, 25, 29, *33–35*, 61; **6:** 24, 26, 30, 41–42, 58; **7:** 37, 40, 48, 52; **8:** 46; **10:** *57*

Hobkirk's Hill (S.C.), battle **9:** 59–60, 62

Hopkins, Esek **7:** *13*, 15–16

Horses; see also Cavalry **3:** *20*, 22; **4:** 9–10; **5:** 29, 58; **6:** 19; **8:** 49, 53

Howard, John **9:** 34, 39, 42

Howe, Richard **4:** 21, 29–*30*; **6:** 19; **7:** 35, 40, 43, *58–60*; **10:** *67*

Howe, Robert **7:** 65–66

Howe, William **2:** 55, 60–61, 63; **3:** 10–11, 37, 42, 44; **4:** 6, 11, 14, 21–22, 25, 27, 29, 36, 38–40, 42–43, 62–63, 66; **5:** 6–7, 9–11, 26, 56; **6:** 9–13, 16–19, 22, 25, 28–31, 33, 35–36, 41, *56–57*, 60; **10:** *67*

Hubbardton (N.Y.), battle **5:** 24–25, 32

Huddy, Joshua **10:** 24

Hudson Highlands **4:** 42; **5:** 11, 48, 55–57; **6:** 8; **8:** 37; **9:** 11–12, 14

Hudson River **4:** 21–24, 40, 42–43, 52, 63; **5:** 7, 10–11, 16, 27–29, 40, 45–48, 51, 55, 57–59; **6:** 8, 12, 16; **8:** 37, 39; **9:** 11; **10:** 10

Huger, Isaac **9:** 59–60

Hutchinson, Thomas **1:** 40

Illinois

    Kaskaskia **8:** 13

Indians; see Native Americans

Indiana

    Vincennes **8:** 13–15

Ireland **3:** 54; **4:** 12; **7:** 33

Iroquois; see also Native Americans **5:** 17; **8:** 16–18, 23, 25–26; **10:** 49–50

Jasper, William **3:** *58–59*; **8:** 31

Jay, John **4:** 32; **10:** 31, 39, *44–45*

Jefferson, Thomas **1:** 44; **2:** 46; **3:** 61–62; **9:** 27; **10:** 34–35

Johnson, Guy **8:** 18

Johnson, William **8:** 18

Jones, David **5:** 32

Jones, John Paul **7:** *20–22*, 24, 26–27, 30–32; **10:** *41*

de Kalb **6:** 20–21; **8:** 55, *59–60*

Kaskaskia (Ill.) **8:** 13

Kettle Creek (Ga.), battle **7:** 67–68

Kentucky **8:** 7–8, 11, 13, 15–16; **10:** 42–43
King's Mountain (S.C.), battle **9:** 20–24
Knowlton, Thomas **2:** 58, 60–61, 66; **4:** 34
Knox, Henry **3:** 23, 37–41; **4:** 53, 66; **6:** *19–20*, 22; **7:** *55*; **10:** 39, 50, *63*
Knyphausen, Wilhelm **6:** 23, 25, 27; **7:** 44, 52; **8:** 49
Kosciuszko, Thaddeus **5:** 20, *48*; **6:** 21

Lafayette, Marquis de **6:** *20–22*, 28; **7:** 36, 47, 50, 59; **8:** 19, 66; **9:** 27; **10:** 11–12, 18, 57, *63*
Lake Champlain; see also Valcour Island **1:** 31, 34; **2:** 50; **4:** 16–21; **5:** 14, 20–21, 23
Lake George **1:** *30–31*, 34; **5:** 28–29
Landais, Pierre **7:** 30
Langdon, John **2:** 11
Laurens, Henry **6:** *34*; **10:** 31
Learned, Ebenezer **5:** 61
Lee, Arthur **6:** 61
Lee, Charles **3:** 12, 15, *55–56*; **4:** 40–41, 46–50, 52; **7:** 46–48, 50–52, 54, *56–57*
Lee, Henry **6:** 53; **8:** *39–40*; **9:** 27, 29–30, *48–49*, 59, 63–64, 68
Lee, Richard Henry **3:** 62; **6:** 43; **10:** *38–39*
Lee, William **7:** 36
Leslie, Thomas **2:** 12–13, *14*, 17
Lewis, Francis **3:** 61
Lexington (Mass.), battle **2:** 16, 18–19, 24–44
Lillington, Alexander **3:** 51
Lincoln, Benjamin **5:** 26, *32–33*, 48, 58, 60; **7:** 66–68; **8:** *28*, 30–31, 50–53, 65; **10:** 9
Livingston, Robert **3:** 62
London **1:** *14–15*, 41
Long, Pierce **5:** 23
Long Island (N.Y.), campaign **4:** 22–29; **5:** 13
Louis XVI, King **6:** 63–65
Lovell, Solomon **8:** 41
Loyalists **1:** 7, 62–63; **2:** 6, 52; **3:** 44, 48, 51, 53, 59, 64; **4:** 29, 50, 55; **5:** 9–10, 16–17, 30, 33, 45, 56, 58, 60; **6:** 10–11, 13, 26–27, 34–35, 60; **7:** 40, 43–44, 48, 62–63, 66–68; **8:** 12, 18–19, 22, 25, 52, 60–62, 64; **9:** 16, 18, 23–24, 35, 48–49, 58–59, 62–64, 67; **10:** 24–25, 32–33, 48, 51–54, 57, 61

MacArthur, Archibald **9:** 42
Madison, James **10:** 39, *63*
Maine **3:** 26, 30–31; **8:** 40–42

Maham, Hezekiah **9:** 59
Marblehead Regiment **4:** 27–28, 38, 53
Marion, Francis **8:** 31; **9:** 29–31, 58–59, *61*, 63, 68
Marshall, John **3:** 48; **8:** 59
Martin, Joseph **8:** 47
Martin, Josiah **3:** 49–50, *55*
Maryland **1:** 12; **2:** 6, 51; **4:** 46, 49; **9:** 27; **10:** 33, 35
Massachusetts **1:** 54–56, 59–60; **2:** 6, 11, 18, 55; **7:** 18; **8:** 40
Boston **1:** 9, 41–45, 52–55, 57, 62–63; **2:** 12–13, 18–19, 22–23, 42, 45, 51, 53–55; **3:** 10, 15, 23, 36–45; **8:** 40
Cambridge **2:** 20, 22; **3:** 12–13, 26
Committee of Safety **2:** 6, 12, 18–20, 45, 55
Provincial Congress **2:** 6, 18, 47, 50; **3:** 11; **5:** 17
Salem **2:** 12–13, *14–15*, 16–17
Maxwell, William **6:** 25; **8:** 23
McCrea, Jane **5:** 31–33, 45, 58
McHenry, James **10:** 39
McLane, Allan **6:** 59
Medicine **2:** 42–43; **8:** 65, 67
Mercenaries, German; see Hessians
Mercer, Hugh **4:** 56, 59–61
Michigan
Detroit **8:** 9, 15
Mifflin, Thomas **4:** *52*; **6:** 43; **7:** 47
Military discipline **2:** 48–49; **3:** 15, 19; **4:** 44; **6:** 25, 55, 59; **8:** 25, 65–66; **9:** 27–28; **10:** 8
Military planning
American **3:** 41; **4:** 34–35, 53, 58; **5:** 11, 55; **6:** 5, 36–37; **7:** 50; **8:** 23, 52; **9:** 30–32, 34, 58, 62; **10:** 10
British **4:** 12–14, 21; **5:** 7, 9–11, 14, 26, 57; **6:** 9–11, 16, 23; **7:** 33–35, 38, 43, 59, 61–65, 68; **8:** 52, 54; **9:** 31, 44; **10:** 12
Militia; see also Minutemen **1:** 19, 22, 25, 60; **2:** 6–7, 10, 12, 16–18, 21–22, 26, 28–29, 53–54, 63, 66; **3:** 13, 36, 47–49, 51–53, 66; **4:** 33, 39–40, 43, 45, 48; **5:** 26, 30, 32–33, 36, 41, 45, 48, 58; **6:** 14, 19, 24–25; **7:** 36–37, 59, 63, 67–68; **8:** 13–15, 19, 28, 41, 50, 55, 57, 59; **9:** 10, 18–19, 32, 34–35, 38–40, 42, 47–48, 51; **10:** 16, 39–40, 51, 57
Minutemen; see also Militia **2:** 6, 17, 24–28, 32, 35; **5:** 17

Mississippi River **1:** 21; **8:** 11–14, 31; **10:** 32, 38, 50

Mohawk Valley **5:** 14, 18, 40, 44, 46; **6:** 9; **8:** 23–24

Monck's Corner (S.C.), battle **8:** 52–53

Monckton, Henry **7:** 55

Monmouth Court House (N.J.), battle **7:** 50–57; **8:** 19

Monongahela River **1:** 22, 29; **2:** 11

Monroe, James **4:** 56–57

Montgomery, Richard **3:** 12, 25–26, 28–35, 37; **4:** 15

Moore's Creek (N.C.), battle **3:** 50–53, 55

Morale **3:** 59; **4:** 31, 35, 43, 63; **5:** 31, 66; **6:** 11, 33; **8:** 39–40, 55

Morgan, Daniel **1:** 29; **3:** 18, 26, 34–*35*; **5:** 26, 51–*52*, 60–61; **8:** 19, 24; **9:** 30–32, 34–35, 38–39, 42, 44, 46, 49–50; **10:** 57, *64*

Morris, Gouverneur **10:** 39

Morris, Robert **10:** 8–9, 39

Moultrie, William **3:** 56

Munroe, William **2:** 25–26

Murray, John, Earl of Dunmore **3:** 46–49

Muskets; see Weapons

Mutiny **8:** 65–66; **10:** 6–8

Native Americans; see also Iroquois; Oneidas **1:** 18, *19–23*, 25, *26–27*, 29, 31, *32–33*, 37, 59; **2:** 51, 53; **5:** *17–19*, 20, 23, 30–32, 40–42, 45, 48; **7:** 65; **8:** 6–11, 14–26; **9:** 19, 34; **10:** 43, 48–50

Negroes; see African Americans

New England **1:** 56; **2:** 18, 51; **3:** 11–12, 46; **4:** 13, 47, 63; **5:** 7, 26, 28, 32, 43; **7:** : 13, 63; **8:** 40; **10:** 8

New France; see also Canada **1:** 20–21, 31

New Hampshire **2:** 6, 10–11, 54; **5:** 13–17, 30, 33

New Jersey **4:** 42, 47–50, 53, 62; **5:** 9; **6:** 8–12, 36, 41, 50; **7:** 43–44, 49, 51–57; **8:** 48; **10:** 8, 24

    Morristown **4:** 61; **5:** 6, 11; **6:** 8, 11; **8:** *44–45*, 47, 65; **9:** 8; **10:** 57

    Princeton **4:** 54, 58–61

    Trenton **4:** 53–58, 61

New York **1:** 9;31, 34, 40–41, 50–51, 53, 57, 60; **2:** 43, 47, 51; **3:** 40, 59; **4:** 18–19, 21–43, 62–64; **5:** 6–7, 9–11, 14–18, 20–32, 40–46,

48–67; **6:** 8, 10, 16, 66; **7:** 37, 41, 43, 56–59, 61, 65; **8:** 16–26, 34–35, 37, 39, 42, 48–49; **9:** 6, 8, 10–11; **10:** 6, 8, 10, 12–13, 25–26

    Albany **5:** 14, 16, 26–27, 29, 46–48, 57

    Burning of **4:** 36–37

    Manhattan **4:** 31–33, 38

    Oswego **5:** 18, 40

    West Point **5:** 57; **9:** 8, 11–14

Newburgh (N.Y.) Addresses **10:** 29–31

Ninety–Six (S.C.), siege **9:** 64–65

North, Frederick **1:** 48–49; **2:** 18; **3:** 6, 8–9; **4:** 63; **5:** 6; **6:** 66–67; **7:** 62; **10:** 22–23, 31

North Carolina **3:** 49–53; **8:** 60–63, 65; **9:** 16, 18, 24, 27, 44, 47, 58, 68; **10:** 12

O'Hara, Charles **9:** 45; **10:** 22

Ohio **10:** 43, 46, 48–49

Ohio Company **1:** 22

Ohio River **1:** 22, 56; **8:** 7–8, 11

Old World; see also Europe **1:** 8, 18

Olive Branch Petition **2:** 52

Oneidas; see also Native Americans **5:** 18; **8:** 17–19; **10:** 50

Oriskany (N.Y.), battle **5:** 41–43, 45

Otis, James **1:** 41

Over–Mountain Men **9:** 19–24

Paine, Thomas **4:** 50–52; **10:** *64*

Paoli (Pa.), battle **6:** 31–33

Parker, John **2:** 27–29

Parker, Jonas **2:** 28

Parker, Peter **3:** 55, 59

Parliament **1:** 15, 37–39, 41–42, 45, 50, 54–55, 60; **2:** 18–19; **3:** 8–9; **6:** 66; **10:** 22–23

Partisans; see also Guerillas **8:** 62, 64; **9:** 29–30, 58–61, 64

Paulus Hook (N.J.), battle **8:** 39–40, 42

Peace conference, 1776 **4:** 29–30

Peace treaty; see Treaty of Paris

Pearson, Richard **7:** 26

Penn, Richard **2:** 52

Pennsylvania **1:** 22, 29; **2:** 51; **4:** 52; **6:** 23–28, 41, 43, 50; **7:** 43; **8:** 7, 16, 19–21, 23–24; **9:** 12, 27; **10:** 7–8

    Philadelphia **1:** 6–7, 9, *10–11*, *12–13*, 50–51, 53, 57–58, 59; **2:** 43, 46–*47*; **4:** 49; **5:** 10, 26; **6:** 8, 11, 14, 17, 19, 29–31, 33–35, 42, 50, 56–60, 66; **7:** 20, 40–41, 43–44,

47–48, 68; **8:** 48; **9:** 6, 12; **10:** 8, 39, 65
Valley Forge **6:** 45–57, 60; **7:** 45–47, 52, 56;
   8: 19, 47, 65–66; **10:** 57
Wyoming Valley **8:** 19, *20–21*
Penobscot Bay (Maine), battle **8:** 40–42
Pepperell, William **1:** 18
Percy, Hugh **2:** 36–38, 44
Phillips, William **5:** 21; **10:** 11–12
Pickens, Andrew **7:** 67–68; **9:** 34, 38, 42, 58, 63
Pickering, Timothy **2:** 12, *16;* **10:** 9, 39
Pigot, Robert **2:** 61, 63
Pitcairn, John **2:** 26–29, 63, 65
"Pitcher," Molly **7:** *57*
Pollard, Asa **2:** 57
Pomeroy, Seth **2:** *59*
Pontiac's War **1:** 37
Poor, Enoch **5:** 60; **8:** 24
Poor, Salem **7:** 36
Population **1:** 9, 11, 14; **3:** 64; **6:** 67; **7:** 63;
   8: 17; **10:** 46–47, 53
Prescott, William **2:** 57–58, 66
Prevost, Augustine **7:** 65, 67; **8:** 27–29
Princeton (N.J.), battle **4:** 58–61, *64–65;* **5:** 7,
   10, 13; **6:** 6–7; **7:** 55
Prisoners **3:** 60; **4:** 41, 43; **5:** 38, 48, 64–65;
   6: 35; **7:** 23, 31, 67–68; **9:** 24; **10:** 24–25
Privateers **7:** 17–19; **8:** 40
Propaganda **2:** 43
Pulaski, Casimir **6:** *21;* **8:** *31*
Putnam, Israel **1:** 29; **2:** *45, 59,* 61, 66; **3:** 15;
   4: 24–25, 32–33
Pyle, John **9:** 48

Quakers **1:** 12; **6:** 34; **9:** 26; **10:** 44
Quebec, see Canada
Quincy, Josiah **1:** 44

Rall, Johann **4:** 53, *55–56*
Ranger **7:** 20, *22–23,* 33
Rations; see Supplies, military
Rawdon, Francis **9:** 59–60, 62–65
Recruiting **4:** 12, 44–45, 58; **6:** 6, 8; **7:** 9, 17,
   19; **8:** 66; **9:** 27
Redcoats; see British armed forces
Reed, Joseph **4:** 34; **9:** 27
"Regulators" **1:** 49; **3:** 50–51, 55
Revere, Paul **1:** 53, 57, 59; **2:** 10, 16, *18–26,*
   28; **8:** 41

Rhode Island **1:** 19, 41, 47; **2:** 6, 54; **6:** 28;
   7: 41, 56–57, 60–61; **8:** 50; **9:** 6, 26
Newport **1:** 9; **4:** 48, 64; **5:** 7; **6:** 10;
   7: 59–61; **8:** 28, 30–31, 49; **9:** 6, 9–10;
   10: 9, 11
Richardson, Richard **3:** 53
Riedesel, Friedrich **5:** *20,* 23, 25, 29–30, 51, 54
Riedesel, Baroness Friederika **8:** 46
Rifles; see Weapons
Robertson, James **8:** 61
Rochambeau, Jean **9:** 6, *9–10;* **10:** 9–10, 13, 18,
   58, *64*
Rockingham, Charles **3:** 8–9
Ross, Elizabeth (Betsy) **6:** 10
Royal governors **1:** 14–15, 22, 44, 49, 51,
   53–54; **2:** 11; **3:** 46–47, 49–50, 55; **5:** 7; **8:** 61
Royal Navy **1:** 29, 38, 47; **2:** 57; **3:** 54–56, 59;
   4: 6, 12, 18, 25, 27, 39, 65–66; **5:** 58; **6:** 17,
   66; **7:** 6–11, 17, 20, 32–33, 60–61, 63, 65;
   8: 28, 32–33, 42, 52, 54; **9:** 8, 11, 58;
   10: 11–13, 15
Ruggles, Timothy **1:** 63
Rules of war **8:** 61–62; **9:** 14–15; **10:** 52
Quarter **8:** 53–54; **9:** 24
Rush, Benjamin **6:** 43–44; **10:** 44
Rutledge, Edward **4:** *29–30*
Rutledge, John **3:** *56;* **8:** 50

Saltonstall, Dudley **8:** 40–42
Sandwich, John **7:** 6, 33, 35
St. Clair, Arthur **5:** *20–21,* 24–25
St. Lawrence River **1:** 31, 35; **3:** 31–32; **4:** 15;
   5: 14
St. Leger, Barry **5:** 14, 18, *40–42,* 45
Saratoga (N.Y.), battles **5:** 48–67; **6:** 41, 43, 63;
   7: 68; **8:** 17; **9:** 11; **10:** 57
Savannah (Ga.), siege **8:** 29–31
Scammell, Alexander **10:** 16
Schuyler, Philip **3:** 24–26; **5:** 26–29, 31, 43–45;
   8: 17
Settlers
British **1:** 18–19, 21, 29, 33; **5:** 17; **8:** 6, 8
French **1:** 20–21, 29; **8:** 6
Seven Years' War **1:** 35; **3:** 6; **7:** 39, 41
Sevier, John **9:** 19
Shelburne, William **10:** 31
Sherman, Roger **3:** 61–62
Ships **1:** 9, 47; **4:** 8–10, 17–19, 22, 65–66;

7: 6–19, 26, 39, 60, 62; **8:** 29, 32, 42–43, 49; **10:** 21
Skenesboro (N.Y.), battle **5:** 21, 23–25
Slave trade **1:** *13*; **10:** 44–45
Slavery **1:** 12–13; **7:** 37; **10:** 44–47, 63
Smallwood, William **9:** *26*
Smith, Francis **2:** 21–23, 35–36
Smith, Jeremiah **1:** 33
Smuggling **1:** 38, 47, 52
Sons of Liberty **1:** 41–42, 44, 53, 63
South Carolina **3:** 53; **4:** 13; **8:** 61, 63, 65; **9:** 16, 30–32, 44, 58–59, 62–63, 65; **10:** 12, 45, 50
  Charleston **1:** 12, 41, 53; **2:** 43; **3:** 46, 54–59; **7:** 63, 66; **8:** 28, 31, 48–54, 56–57, 62; **9:** 68; **10:** 25, 52
Spain **5:** 13; **6:** 65; **7:** 33, 38; **8:** 31–34; **10:** 36, 38
Spies **2:** 12, 18–20, 23, 55; **4:** 40, 59; **5:** 13, 23; **7:** 36; **9:** 12, 14–15
Stark, John **2:** *58*, 61; **5:** 30, 32–36, 38, 64
Starvation **3:** 31, 64–66; **4:** 41; **5:** 58; **6:** 48–49; **8:** 47, 65–66; **9:** 9; **10:** 8
State troops **6:** 37; **9:** 35
Stephen, Adam **6:** 24, 27
Steuben, Friedrich **6:** 21, 53–55; **7:** 47, 55–56; **8:** 47; **9:** 15, 27; **10:** 57, *65*
Stevens, Edward **9:** 47, 50
Stewart, Alexander **9:** 64, 67
Stony Point, (N.Y.), battle **8:** 37–39
Strategy; see Military planning
Submarine *Turtle* **4:** 37–38
Sullivan, John **2:** *10–11*; **4:** 16–17, 24, 29, 52; **6:** 20, 24–25, 27; **7:** 59–60; **8:** *23–26*, 30; **10:** 49
Sumter, Thomas **8:** 62, 64; **9:** 58–59, 63–64
Supplies, military **2:** 7, 12; **3:** 31, 40, 44, 63–66; **4:** 6–9, 11, 16–17; **5:** 13, 16, 29–30, 46, 48, 56; **6:** 14, 30, 42, 45, 48–53, 62; **7:** 44–45, 67; **8:** 42–43, 47, 57, 65–67; **9:** 9, 27, 44–45, 58; **10:** 6, 8, 26, 29

Tactics, see Military Planning
Tarleton, Banastre **8:** 52, 53–54, 59, 62, 64; **9:** 24, 31–32, 34–36, 38–39, 42–44, 48; **10:** *67*
Taxes **1:** 36–42, 47, 50; **3:** 9; **6:** 66; **10:** 40
Tennessee **10:** 42–43

Thayendanegea; see Brant, Joseph
Thomson, William **3:** 53
Tilghman, Tench **6:** 22; **10:** 28
Tories; see Loyalists
Trade **1:** 11–12, 14, 37–38, 42, 47–50, 57; **2:** 14, 18; **3:** 63–64; **7:** 38, 63–64; **8:** 17, 28; **10:** 36, 38
Training, military **2:** 48–49; **6:** 53–55; **7:** 47, 52
Trappers **2:** 21, 22; **8:** 6
Treaty of Paris **10:** 31–32, 47–49
Trenton (N.J.), battle **4:** 53–57; **5:** 7, 10, 13; **6:** 6–7
Trumbull, John **2:** 17, 53; **5:** 20
Tryon, William **1:** 49, 51
Turner, Nat **10:** 46

Uniforms **1:** 26, *36–37*; **2:** *6–7, 17, 19*; **3:** *9, 11, 14, 17–18, 20*; **4:** *10, 13, 22, 48, 53*; **5:** *11, 24–25, 33*; **6:** *9, 22, 25–26, 37*; **7:** : *61*; **8:** *43, 47*; **9:** *34, 36–37*; **10:** *14*

Valcour Island **4:** 17–21
Vergennes, Charles **5:** 12–13; **6:** 62–64; **8:** 32
Vermont **2:** 50; **5:** 30, 32–39, 48
Veterans **10:** 42–43, 57
Vincennes (Ind.) **8:** 13–15
Virginia **1:** 8, 12, *19*, 22, 29, 33, 40, 44, 56, 58; **2:** 6, 51–52; **3:** 11–12, 46–49; **8:** 11, 15; **9:** 18, 27, 31; **10:** 10–13, 46, 61–62
  Mount Vernon **1:** 20–21; **3:** 12; **10:** *15*, 65
  Norfolk **3:** 46–49
  Riflemen, Virginia **3:** 18, 26, 34–35; **5:** 51–52; **9:** *34*
  Yorktown **10:** 12, 16
Virginia Capes, battle **10:** 13, 15

Walton, George **3:** 61
War of 1812 **10:** 47–48, *50*, 63
Ward, Artemas **2:** 53, 55, 58; **3:** 15, 38
Warner, Seth **3:** 28; **5:** 24–25, 32, 35
Warren, Joseph **2:** 47, 59–60, 65
Washington, D.C. **10:** 65
Washington, George **1:** 20–25, 28–29; **2:** 46–47, 52; **3:** 11–*12*, 13–15, 26, 36, 38, 40–41, 44, 66; **4:** 22–28, 31–40, 42–50, 52–53, 55–63; **5:** 6, 10–11, 26, 33; **6:** 6–9, *11–16*, 19, 21, 24–25, 27–29, 36–38, 40–44, 46–48, *51–55*, 63–67; **7:** 11, 36, 41, 45–52, 54–59, 61, 68;

8: 19, 23, 26, 37–39, 42–43, 46–47, 55,
  65–67; **9:** 8–10, 14–15, 26–28; **10:** 6, 8–*13*,
  16, 18, 24–29, 31, 33, 35, 38–42, 52, 54–55,
  57–58, *65*
Washington, Martha   **6:** *57*; **10:** *65*
Washington, William   **4:** 56, 66; **9:** *35*, 39–41,
  43, *54*
Wayne, Anthony   **6:** 24, 30, *31*–32, 38–40, 53;
  7: 50, *55*; **8:** *36*–*39*; **10:** 8, 12, 25
Waxhaws (S.C.), battle   **8:** 54–*55*; **9:** 24, 41
Weapons
  Bayonets   **2:** 49, 62, 65; **6:** 31; **9:** 38
  Cannons/Artillery pieces   **2:** *16*; **3:** 22–23;
    4: 53; **5:** 21, 57, 60; **7:** 7, 26, 49; **10:** 58
  Gunpowder   **4:** 66
  Muskets   **2:** 48–49; **3:** 16–*18*; **7:** *12*; **9:** 27
  Pistols   **3:** *21*
  Rifles   **3:** 17–*18*
  Sabers/Swords   **3:** *21*
West Indies   **1:** 9, 37, 57; **2:** 18; **3:** 63; **4:** 66;
  7: 16, 37–38, 43, 64; **8:** 28–29, 31, 33–34;
  9: 6, 10; **10:** 25–26, 36, 53
Whipple, Abraham   **1:** 48–49; **8:** *50*, 52
Whipple, Prince   **4:** *55*
White, Philip   **10:** 24
White Plains (N.Y.), battle   **4:** 39–40
Wilderness   **1:** 21, 28, 31; **8:** 8
Wilkes, John   **3:** *8*
Wilkinson, James   **5:** 53, *60*, 62
Willett, Marinus   **5:** 42

Williams, Otho Holland   **9:** *47*
Winter quarters   **4:** 50, 61; **5:** 6, 11; **6:** 8, 45–60;
  8: 14, 42–45, 47, 65; **9:** 8–9; **10:** 6, 8, 29
Wolfe, James   **1:** 35
Women
  Acland, Lady Harriet   **5:** *61*
  Adams, Abigail   **10:** 60
  Arnold, Peggy (Shippen)   **7:** *48*; **10:** 60
  Hart, Nancy   **8:** 64
  McCrea, Jane   **5:** 31–33, 45, 58
  "Molly Pitcher"   **7:** *57*
  Mrs. Motte   **9:** 62–63
  Mrs. Murray story   **4:** *33*
  Riedesel, Baroness Friederika   **8:** 46
  Ross, Elizabeth (Betsy)   **6:** *10*
  Traveling with armies   **4:** 9–10; **5:** 20, 61;
    8: 46
  Washington, Martha   **6:** *57*; **10:** 65
Woodford, William   **3:** 48–49
Wooster, David   **6:** 13
Wyoming (Pa.) "Massacre"   **8:** 19–21

Yorktown (Va.), Siege   **10:** 16–23, 58
Yost, Hon   **5:** 45

Acknowledgments

Architect of the Capitol: Front cover, 22, 23, 35, 40
Author's collection: 59B
Anne S. K. Brown Military Collection, John Hay Library, Brown University, Providence, Rhode Island: 24,
  32–33, 34, 41, 54
Colonial Williamsburg Foundation: 32
Independence National Historical Park: 39, 48, 62, 63C, 63B, 64T, 64B, 65T
Library of Congress: 9, 11, 13T, 16, 18, 19, 27T, 27B, 28, 29, 34T, 42–43, 44–45, 46, 49, 50–51, 52, 56,
  58, 60, 61, 63T, 64C, 65B, 66, 67
The Senate of the Commonwealth of Virginia, courtesy Library of Virginia: 20–21
Military Archive & Research Services, England: 14, 30, 37
National Archives: 8, 15T, 15B, 38, 44, 55
National Park Service: 6–7 painting by Don Troiani
Naval Historical Center, Washing ton, D.C.: 25, 26
U.S. Government Printing Office: 43T (flag), 59T

Map by Jerry Malone